Lord, Have Mercy!

Give Us Grace and

Grandma's Cornbread!

Created by

Priscilla Y. Hill

ISBN: 0984398104

EAN-13: 9780984398102

All proceeds to be given to New Covenant United Church of Christ

Photographs: Priscilla Y. Hill

Illustrations: Inspired by Priscilla Y. Hill; Illustrated by Garry Collins of Locust Street Art Classes, Inc.

Logo: Gibran McNeal

Thank you, Betsy Gordon, Senior Editor & Wicked Sunny, Senior Designer of PublishingGurus.com, who, with love and care, helped bring this book into full bloom.

Printed and bound in the United States of America

Books and Articles by Priscilla Y. Hill

Poetry: "Back in the Day," A Chapbook, 2003

Article: " Level Playing Field," 1999, <u>Buffalo News</u>

Article: "Rising Prices a Good Thing," 2008, <u>Buffalo News</u>

Contributory Letter: "Go, Tell Michelle," 2009

ACKNOWLEDGEMENTS

To my Lord, who is my strength, my refuge and my joy!

So many people have had an influence on the completion of this first book.

I'd love to acknowledge, first, my prayer partner, friend, sister, and the person who inspired me to see this book through. Her prayers, her presence, and her persistence have given me the confidence and courage to bring this book to fruition. Thank you, Marilyn Gault.

I would like to acknowledge my Pastor, Rev. Will J. Brown, for his insight into the world as it turns, for his guidance and spiritual support.

Thank you, my daughters, Chari and Gina, Nanette, and granddaughter Ashley. You have always been so supportive and encouraging to me, reading my "stuff" and giving me constructive criticism. To Ian, who keeps me writing letters.

My thanks to Gary Earl Ross, who taught me to look over and through, teaching me what I needed to know in his workshops.

I'd like to acknowledge the East High School Writing Group of students and Faculty: Mrs. Fenton, Martha Marks and Jeffrey, who visited my church and listened, like Daquan, who quietly paid attention to my poems and liked them. Thanks especially to Davion, who critiqued "An Ode to a Pen" so succinctly and obviously that it startled me. How intelligent, spiritual, and self-assured you are, Davion! God bless. And I cannot thank Greg and Karen enough for giving me those "Kozak" moments.

Also, I thank the guys who sit at the table in the back of the Fellowship Hall, telling stories of their days driving the city busses. That's where my bus-driver stories came from. Thanks, Al, Charles, Shelton and Hank, whose humor keeps us laughing.

I especially thank with a loving heart those members who took time to write something special for all of us: Helen, Maxine, Chari, Patrick, Eleanor, Marilyn, and those ladies who contributed to "Remember…"

Peace and Love, Priscilla

DEDICATION

To God Be the Glory! To You I dedicate this book.

I am blessed to be able to take a journey over more than thirty years, from Salem Church to New Covenant UCC, from a dark path to one of enlightenment.

I am grateful that the Lord has guided me through and somehow kept me on the right path, using me in His own special way, through this gift of writing.

I dedicate this book to the Congregation of New Covenant United Church of Christ, Buffalo, NY: to those who are still there struggling, keeping the faith, lifting us up to God's glory; and to the Shepherd who guides us, teaches us God's Word each day, Pastor, Rev. Will J. Brown; and to those who have gone on to a greater glory.

These pages are in memory of my late family members: Eloise Green McPherson, Ma (Poo-Poo), Claude McPherson (Mac), Richard Green, Jr., and my late father, Richard Green, Sr. In honor of my present family: brother Mark, my daughters, Charisse and Regina, grandchildren Gibran,(Mildred) Ashley, and Julian; and my great-grandson, Kahlile. Also, my new family: Adriane, Cathy and grandson, Clinton (Trey). My Diva friends who still hold me close in friendship and good food: Carolyn, Sonia, Erlene, Denise, Barbara, Althea and Vinnette; my Mary B. Talbert Civic and Cultural Club; and the Uncrowned Queens.

My close friends: Loreda, who loves to dance and talk; Lola, who loves me no matter what; and Nanette, who reminds me to "Never let them take away your Joy!"
To my husband Wiley, who has been so supportive and loving; taking care of me each day and filling me with the passion I've longed for.

Love you all… Priscilla, Cilla, P, Lala, Mom, Ma

TABLE OF CONTENTS

STEP I   NEW COVENANT CELEBRATIONS!
THE FIRST INGREDIENTS

These poems were written as part of celebrations at New Covenant United Church of Christ. Most were for Church and Pastor Anniversaries. Others are contributions from members of our Church; remembering departed loved ones and members who helped to build our foundation. The short stories were added as a wonderful surprise, when you need a break. I hope you will sit back and enjoy our feast, in Step I and II, spiced with the best ingredients and special flavors…with love.

Ephesians 2:5
"For it is by Grace you have been saved, through faith and this is not from yourselves; it is a gift from God"

HISTORY OF NEW COVENANT UNITED CHURCH OF CHRIST

Twenty-eight people came from Bethel African Methodist Episcopal (AME) Church, near Michigan Avenue. That was a "red light" district then, and some members wanted to move because they didn't want the children to pass through this area.

They worshipped together for a while. Some wanted to remain AME; they formed St. Luke AME Zion. Mr. Wright, Mrs. Ridley, Mr. Lloyd, and remaining members formed Lloyd's Congregational Church. The Church was named after Mr. Lloyd, because he mortgaged his home so the group would have a place to worship.

In 1958, Lloyd's Congregational joined the newly-formed United Church of Christ. In 1974, Lloyd's UCC merged with St. Peter's UCC and became New Covenant UCC. During this same period, a significant number of members of Salem UCC joined with New Covenant UCC.

After Bethany UCC burned down, that congregation held joint worship services with Concordia Lutheran Church. This arrangement continued for ten to fifteen years. Eventually, members of Bethany UCC united with New Covenant.

New Covenant United Church of Christ

NEW COVENANT FAMILY DAY
May 24, 2009

"Our Family defines who we are. When one part hurts, we all feel the pain."

Coming together on this special day
Our New Covenant Family is here to stay
Honoring our folks for the good deeds done
Celebrating lives already won

OUR

Look at us now, all smiles on our faces
Getting ready to really go places
Here you get a straight look in the eye
A fine, firm handshake and warm goodbye
A quick hug, maybe a kiss on the cheek
Is sometimes what we need and subtly seek

FAMILY

When we laugh out loud at Rev. Brown's jokes
And listen to the stories of the older folks
Or smell a family's ministry
Lingering throughout the Sanctuary
When we sit and pray at someone's bedside
Or feel the Lord's presence at a marriage with pride
And especially a Going Home ce-re-mo-ny
With loved ones in mournful har-mo-ny

DEFINES

Oh, we are wonderfully and marvelously made so nice
By the Father of Jesus who bought us twice
Our children we show them how important they are
Hoping they won't stray too very far
Books of the Bible they do recite
Learning the Word with all their might
Looking and doing, oh so fine

As they usher in the Lord's sunshine

WHO

Through anniversaries, births, deaths, baptism and strife
We celebrate the cycle of life
With stirring sermons, spirited singing, cool cookouts and cookins
We celebrate the cycle of life within.

WE

Older folks' memories grow dimmer in many a way,
Like "Oh, I think I used to know them, back in the day"
These generational builders prayed a lot
Sang, worked, sweated and taught us on the spot
"What you do speaks so loud, no one can hear what you say"
and, "Always kiss them goodnight! Amen."

ARE

"Our Family defines who we are and what we will become!"

CELEBRATING THIRTY-TWO YEARS

Thirty-two years ago the Lord
Had a plan and a promise
Of four churches coming together
Who didn't know whether
They'd even stay together

But the Lord had a plan and a promise

Mr. Lloyd mortgaged his house
Then St. Peter's came about
For this beginning meant
A brand-new New Covenant.

Salem came soon from the quagmire
Then Bethany-Concordia arose from the fire
Because the Lord had a plan
And a promise
To bring them together

Four churches…thirty-two years
To the biggest little church
On the corner

With Pastor Will J. Brown
A Baptist Preacher
Who reaches us
And teaches us
God's Word…
Because
The Lord had a plan and a promise
Keeping us together… thirty-two years.

Priscilla Y. Hill …written for the 32nd anniversary of New Covenant

I heard a train whistle one October morning…
THE NEW COVENANT PRAYER TRAIN

Full steam ahead! All aboard!
Step right on up to the platform, y'all,
The Train's a-comin'.
The New Covenant Prayer Train --
Come on! Get on board!
The Engineer gave the signal
To our Conductor
From Matthew 5:13, Psalm 40
And His Holy Book to guide us.
He passed it along to the workers
Who started loading the fuel,
A little bit at a time.
Now the New Covenant Prayer Train
Is full steam ahead.
You can hear the whistle blow
From far away, loud and proud,
Letting everybody know
We are here … ready for our passengers.
Because this is a Spirit-guided prayer train,
Where everyone's got a job to do,
'Cause everyone makes a difference,
Helping our train to run smoother, stronger
And at a good pace,
Ready to even pick up wanderers
Not at the station…
The passengers started to climb aboard,
Anticipating the journey,
Excited about this Christian ride;
Making a joyful noise, singing
"Hallelujah, thine the glory, Hallelujah, amen.
Hallelujah, thine the glory, Revive us again!"
As they put their fares in the cup,
As they joined the prayer warriors
In the Engine Room.

Yes, as they showed humility and service to others,
Helping the mothers with their children,
Guiding people in their wheelchairs,
Mentoring our young folk,
Encouraging them to stay,
Fellowshipping with new passengers,
As they decide if they should take the train or not,
Telling them of this joyous journey.
Yes, everyone's got something to give;
Everyone makes a difference…
We came together over the years
From many directions,
Putting this train together with our beliefs,
Our faith, our prayers, our sweat and tears.
Sometimes a bolt came loose, slowing us down;
But we got our prayer partners
Coming together each day, praying
For guidance, asking the Lord,
What should we do? How should we do it?
And thanking Him for what He has done
He heard us and He is fixing it!
Lord have mercy!…
We're on the right track now,
Still picking up passengers along the way.
Frequently we pause…
Remembering whence we came,
Checking our direction
From the Engineer with the Master plan.
Then it's full steam ahead…
On the New Covenant Prayer Train –
All aboard!   All aboard!   All aboard!
And Amen!

October 19, 2008 New Covenant's 34th Anniversary Homecoming
Celebration.

REV. WILL J. BROWN: MAGNIFICENT POSSIBILITIES

*"The seeds of potential that He has planted among us...
The magnificent possibilities that are opened to us."*

Written by Pastor Brown in the 1995 Annual Report

This Baptist minister from Mississippi
Came to us one silent Sunday
Uplifting our spirits with his presence...

Then... there was a lady named Bernice who said, "Amen, Brown!"
To let him know he was doing okay... in the silence
And everyone stared...
Others shed subtle tears as they sang quiet hymns

He continued teaching us the Word with his intensity
Helping fill our Sanctuary with a joyful noise
On our little corner of the world

He planted the seeds of potential among us
"Putting butterflies of excitement in our stomachs"
Showing us that we could make a difference
That we could grow spiritually, financially and
Become Ambassadors of Christ.

These magnificent possibilities
became our realities
When the seeds he planted in 1980 began to grow
And sprout new life into this Church on the corner
Silent Sundays became "Amens, Hallelujahs, Praise God"
People stood, clapped, cried openly,
praised God with joyful noises;
and he, too, danced in the aisle
 Letting God know we were here

He led us in subtle ways, too, like changing our picnics to cookouts,
Telling us about Fannie Lou Hammer and Mary B. Talbert,

or back in the day,
when he marched for the right to vote,
protesting and spreading the word;
creating possibilities all the while,
In the Mississippi Freedom Democratic Party.

God gave him the vision to see the potential
these seeds had for us,
if we nourish them with faith
stroke them with love and charity
water them with kindness and hard work
then wait and be patient for them to sprout
reaping the rewards; harvesting the possibilities.

He questioned us to stimulate our growth…
He saw us study and asked, "Do you understand?"
He asked the ushers, "Do you want to be the first to welcome?"
He asked the children, "Do you want to play and learn?"
The ladies, "Do you want to walk down those stairs again?
The Deacons, "Do you really want to mind our Spiritual business?"
The Trustees, "Do you want to lead and be Stewards of Tithing?"
The Choir, "Do you want to make a joyful noise?"
He asked the men, "Do you want to sing?"
And his Church family, "What will you give to reach your potential
Of becoming the biggest little Church in this city?"

As we pondered these questions,
One fine day, our Pastor chose a wife,
Who now sits in the first pew;
Who is his backup; his upfront;
And always stands beside him

People smiled.
The answers came quickly…
The possibilities are now limitless…
The seeds are still sprouting…

**Rev. Will J. Brown – God has richly blessed us with your
leadership these 25 years!**

KEYS TO THE KINGDOM

Woke up one morning, jumped out of bed
Trying to remember something I said.

> Cooked a good breakfast,
> Ate all my food,
> Made plans for this day
> In a real good mood.

Couldn't think anymore,
So I pranced out the door;
But I let out a shout --
I locked myself out!

> Walked up the street
> For my girlfriend to meet;
> Maybe she has the key
> For po' little ol' me.

Then I remembered
Why it happened this way:
Lord, please forgive me –
I forgot to pray!

> Lo and behold,
> The right car did I see
> With my girlfriend dangling
> Keys in front of me.

So Lord, thank you for your presence
In my life today,
Guiding me, loving me,
Showing me the way.
But the keys I truly seek
Nearer my heart
Are the keys to Your Kingdom,
So we're never apart.

THE LORD IS AWESOME!

April 22, 2006, Resurrection Sunday

Kneeling here tonight in the darkness
Feeling humbled before the Lord
Remembering I read somewhere
He knew us before we were even born...
Imagine that!
Before....we...were...born.

The Lord is so awesome.
One day He asked Job
"Have you ever given orders to the morning,
Or shown the day its place?" (Job 38: 12)
Whew! The Lord is awesome!

He laid the Earth's foundation
Marking off its dimensions
While the morning stars sang together
And all the Angels shouted for joy (Job 38: 4,7)
The Lord is awesome!

He had a divine plan for us too
Sending His son to live as a man
Among us... showing us His love
Everlasting!
The crowd was fickle and foolish that week
At first they had called Him Messiah.
They had heard about the miracles:
How He healed the sick, touched by the hem
Of His garment; made the blind see,
The lame walk; walked on water
And even raised the dead.
He is so awesome!

They thought He had come to save them
Save them from the Roman soldiers
The crowd questioned:
Where are your armies? Your warriors?
They didn't even understand.

They didn't know that He knew us before...
And came to save us... everlasting!
The crowd was full of hatred now
They jeered Him, beat Him, spat on Him
And called Him names

According to God's plan
They crucified Him high on a hill;
Not knowing what they had done,
To fulfill the Messianic Prophecy
Of Daniel 7:13

Near death, His son cried loudly
"Forgive them, Father!"
Then the crowd fell silent;
They wondered in awe...
As the Son's Spirit was lifted
And the Prophecy fulfilled
The Lord is awesome!

Purchasing our salvation
Giving us a new covenant now
Letting us have a personal relationship
With the Spirit Who intercedes
When we don't know how to pray;
With the Comforter too
When we need healing from pain and suffering
A new covenant
Showing us His love and His Grace
Through everlasting life

Because He knew us before we were
Even born...
And wanted to give us eternity
Whew, the Lord is awesome!

For my Dad at Easter, March 23, 2005

JESUS WEPT

Remembering that little girl of five
all dressed up, ready to say her
first Easter verse, at that little white
Church on Jefferson Avenue.

"Jesus webb," was what she nervously said
and she cried softly
because she didn't know what it meant,
except that Jesus was sad.

And He was sad.
"Oh, Jerusalem," He sobbed.
The people didn't know either...
as they cheered the Messiah,
waving palms in His path
and missing the message.

Jesus wept...
when He saw the destruction
and the devastation of Jerusalem.
They hadn't recognized
the time of His coming,

Or that His mission was guided
by the Scripture,
Or that He was coming for
their salvation...

Or that they would take Him
to the Cross
where He would forgive them
their sins.

Jesus wept...
and she wept too.

GOD IS NOT AN ATM

I saw a young lady at the ATM punch in her pin code. The message read, "No funds available." She said, "And the Bank is closed, too! Oh, Lord, what am I gonna do?"

GOD IS NOT AN ATM

You can't punch in the right code

And get what you want in an instant.

You can't see right away if you have any prayer requests
Waiting to be claimed;
Sometimes you can't see those that have already been given.

You see, GOD IS NOT AN ATM

But you can put a prayer request in
God's Promise Account …with interest.
God will come through:
But you must have faith, belief, and patience
That His promise will be there when you need it.

GOD IS NOT AN ATM

We might get upset and frustrated
If that ATM is not working;
But God is not like that ATM.
We might misunderstand God's timing,
But we know He is not broke.
God is always in control.

We live by faith, not by what we see.
The ATM might not work; the Bank might be closed,
But God is always open,

Always there to receive our prayers of faith.
He is at work, no matter if we see our prayers answered or not…
But they will surely be.

GOD IS NOT AN ATM

When we are troubled and get knocked down with life's trials
God is ready to give His gifts with answered prayer.
He will pick us up, brush us off,
And send us on our way
He is a miracle-working God
In His own time… in His own way.

We are saved by Grace, God's gift to us…

Nothing we do on our own...
Like punch in pin codes at the ATM.

GOD IS NOT AN ATM

October 12, 2007
33rd Homecoming Anniversary

BUS DRIVER #2…. Mr. Charles Sheldon

Mr. Charles Sheldon had only a few hours left. He had eaten the lunch his wife, Louise, had prepared for him, in his favorite aluminum lunch bucket. There was the same Spam, lettuce and tomatoes and lots of mayo, a pickle, an apple and a daily Scripture. His thermos had hot chocolate today.

"She must have been in a good mood or run out of coffee," he thought.

Mr. Sheldon knew this Friday's last run would be the same as always, after forty years driving city busses.

"Nothing ever changes," he said to himself. "Think I'll call Al later, so we can make arrangements for the Fish Dinner Retirement party next week."

This gray December afternoon, winds whipped the two inches of snow around the streets, making it seem colder than it was.

At 2:30 pm, on the corner of Jefferson and Clinton Streets, Sis. Clara McIntosh the 2nd, as she calls herself, waited, fidgeting in the brisk cold. She was bundled in a huge black (or brown, if the sun shined on it) cape over the long, green, military-style coat. Her head was wrapped with a multi-colored wool cap and a reddish scarf around her mouth and neck. The rubber boots Sis. Clara wore were way too big; she sloshed along when she walked.

" Good afternoon, Charlie. May the good Lord take a likin' to ya. Have a good day, in His name, amen."

As she fumbled for the change, which she never seemed to have, in her raggedy blue cloth bag, Mr. Sheldon said, "Get on the bus. Have a seat until you find it."

"God bless you, Charlie. You a kind, Christian man."

Then she started, exactly two minutes later, standing in the aisle next to the third row of seats.

"Hallelujah, Lord. You have been good to me." The same words every week. "I know you been good to these peoples on this bus too."

Mr. Sheldon glared at her as he always did. "Please Sis. Clara McIntosh the 2nd, not today. It's Friday, and my last run. All we want to do is get home in peace."

The blustering snow started to come down hard, settling and clinging on the bus windows, making the wipers work as fast as they could.

Sis. Clara was in the middle of the bus, waving her gleaners, telling funny stories about what happened to some people who didn't put money in the gleaners. One young man, sitting in the back, began looking for quarters, as did most of the fifteen people on the bus.

"Sit down, Sis. Clara," were the last words passengers heard before the bus collided with a tractor-trailer, swerving sideways down Jefferson Avenue near Broadway. It hit the bus dead center, just where Sis. Clara McIntosh the 2nd had been standing.

There was enough room in the aisle for the passengers from the back to climb through, stepping over the crumpled body of Sis. Clara McIntosh the 2nd. Her gleaner lay beside her, filled with quarters.

Mr. Sheldon's heart was heavy as he looked at Sis. Clara's dark face, lined from ages of living, but so smooth and peaceful now.

"Okay, now," said the medic. "Time to get her out of here."

Mr. Sheldon took her gleaners and the blue bag and sat

beside her in the ambulance, holding her hand. Sis Clara squeezed Mr. Sheldon's hand and whispered something in his ear.

"Charlie, ya git all my possessions. Don't let nobody else get 'em. Look all the way through 'em, real good." Then she slipped away with a sigh.

He could still hear her soft, whiny voice, inspiring people and badgering them, too.

"Come on, y'all. Put them quarters in them gleaners. Help somebody who got less than ya. Y'all know ya been blessed this week."

Mr. Sheldon took responsibility for the funeral arrangements of Sis. Clara McIntosh the 2nd, because she had told him she had no family.

"Charlie, you knows ya in my will. Ya gets ten per cent and my church gets the rest, after expenses, ya know." Mr. Sheldon would just nod his head "okay".

"Tomorrow we're going to the church and see what can be done. I know Pastor Brown and the church will help us. Louise, we can help some, but where will the rest come from? We gotta put her away in a proper fashion."

His wife knew what he was feeling. "Baby, you got to put your trust in the Lord! Give it to the Lord in prayer. You always do," as she poured their nightly night caps of Old Grand-Dad and tea with lemon.

"Keeps the haints away," she always said.

The next morning, before the meeting with the Pastor, Mr. Sheldon and Louise sifted thoroughly through Sis. Clara McIntosh the 2nd's coat, dress, bag, and boots. They found what she had left them and an old, battered letter.

The day Sis. Clara wanted for her funeral was a Friday, her favorite. She had written down the songs to be sung and the Scripture from Ephesians 10:13. She wrote, "I want pink roses on a pink casket. I want you to present the check. Remember, after expenses and your ten percent. Keep my word. Yours in God's love, Sis Clara McIntosh the 2nd."

Hundreds of bus riders, hearing of her death, paid her the greatest respect and attended her funeral. People were lined up outside in the street, at the Jefferson Avenue Church where Sis. Clara grew up.

After some people spoke and told Sis. Clara's hilarious stories, the Choir sang her two favorite songs, "Amazing Grace" and "There Will Be Peace in the Valley."

The Pastor introduced Mr. Sheldon solemnly.

"You know I loved this old lady. She loved us all, too, especially her church. At the request of Sis. Clara McIntosh the 2nd, I would like to present to the Jefferson Avenue Church of God in Christ, a check for forty thousand (a hush came over the people), fifty dollars and thirty-seven cents." Everyone jumped up, thanking Sis. Clara McIntosh the 2nd and praising God. The choir sang a joyful, upbeat Spiritual as the funeral procession began to take Sis. Clara McIntosh the 2nd to her final resting place.

"You know you been blessed." Mr. Sheldon could hear her voice in the midst of the praises and hallelujahs.

This story was created from a compilation of stories told by three Bus Drivers at New Covenant Church: Mr. Albert Thompson, Mr. Charles Shallowhorn and Mr. Sheldon Cottrell -- and of course Mr. Hank Sevillian.

LORD, CAN I BE AN ANGEL?

Lord, you know when I'll be coming.
And I have some questions for you,
If You don't mind.

Lord, before I go on my way,
Will you help me in my journey "home?"
Lord, will I see Jesus' face?
And will he look like me?

Lord, can I kinda guide my grandchildren
To the "Road Not Taken"?
To the path that leads to you?
Can I teach them how to pray, Lord?

Lord, can I trip up those nasty girls
Before they get to my grandsons
And show them the right One?

Can I pinch those bad boys
Whenever they smile at my granddaughter,
And guide them to the One who is right?

Lord, can I teach them about faith,
About love, compassion, respect,
And responsibility?

Lord, can I bring my daughters closer together?
Can I soften Gina's technique?
And strengthen Chari's resolve?
Can I comfort them and...
Help them remember you?

Lord, I know I'm asking a lot of you
And I'm not even there yet.

Lord, can I peek into New Covenant

Every once in a while,
To hear the Reverend's words
That bring faith, hope, and tears
To my heart?

Lord, can I hear the Choir sing
"This and That," which makes us
Jump to our feet?

Or the soft, mellow hymns
That bring us peace?

Lord, can I still get busy in Christ,
After I enter the Gate called Beautiful?
And Lord, Lord, can I send them a poem
Every now and then?

GOD'S GIFTS

November 2006
32ⁿᵈ New Covenant Church Anniversary

On this blessed November morning we come
once again to celebrate our presence on this corner of our world.
The Lord knows we all hunger… hunger for the idols
of our day… in this material world
He knows the real hunger is to walk in His presence…
in His Word.
So He has prepared a feast for us
to satisfy that hunger each day.

Our eyes have not seen nor our ears heard;
our minds cannot even comprehend
What a feast Our Lord has prepared for us!
He wants us to join Him at His table.
Oh, feast your eyes on the gifts before you,
Taste the sweetness of the fruits of the Spirit –
Joy, peace, longsuffering, goodness and faithfulness.
Smell the aroma of His loving kindness,
Feel the joy emanating from His love,
Listen… to the sound of His Word!

Abundance of life is waiting for you at this table.
The main entrée is remission of your sins,
Supplied and paid for by His son Jesus the Christ.

You may not see, hear nor understand yet,
but to those who love Him
The Lord will reveal these gifts
…through the Holy Spirit.

So in our little corner of the world,
on this 32ⁿᵈ Anniversary,
Pull up to the table of Grace.

Enjoy, with passion, God's gifts.
Fill yourself with His glory,
And you will be blessed and satisfied.

A GATE CALLED BEAUTIFUL

Did you know there is a gate?
A gate called Beautiful
Where the Lord smiles and miracles happen.

Many footsteps led to the temple
Where people went to pray
And some even asked for silver and gold
Instead the Lord smiled and miracles happened.

A blind man sees the glory of God
A lame man walks, and praises Him
At this gate
This gate called Beautiful.

We, too, are sinners
Travelling in the sands of time
But only by His grace
Do we walk this trembling pace
Tripping and stumbling
Climbing and grumbling

On this journey to the gate
Where we will not ask for riches:
All we ask is that He
Breathes on us,
Opens our hearts with His love,
Touches our lips with His word.

Just don't count us out,
As we seek the magnificence
Of the I AM
The cloud by day
The flame by night
The whisperer of our consciousness
The redeemer of our sins

Who leads us to the gate –
The gate called Beautiful.

A STUDY THEREOF...

I used to see your reverence
Created in a thousand places
Like in the huge church windows
On that Broadway Street corner
Where we skipped school
To throw water on our faces
To light the candles
And pray for somebody.

They made you look so serene
And beautiful, like an angel
With Your hair sparkling
Your eyes seeing right through us.

I saw you in my grandma's house
And all the houses in the Projects
Even my own...
Except you were not hanging on a wall
You were in a small gray book.

We thought it was a Bible
For a long time
But it was a study thereof...
Of old men with lots of hair
Of great wrath and rage
Of life and pain and always death
Of pictures with white people
In solemn poses with praying hands.

My crayon was black
Moving lines that went up and down
Scribbling and looping sometimes

As I flipped through the pages
Looking for myself
Drawing teardrops in Your eyes

Because you were blond and blue.
I used to see many angels
A special one I darkened a bit
Pressing hard till I couldn't even
See her face anymore

I used to wonder sometimes,
When I get to Heaven
Will you look like my daddy or grandpa?
 Or even Uncle Brother?

Will your hair be nappy?
Your skin light? Brown? Black?

They said you are Your Father
They say He is mine too
When I look in the mirror
Will I see you?

So I tried to remember
The prayer Mama taught
When I went to sleep each night
But never said, "If I should die"
Because alone was I and so afraid
Of all the black crayon lines
That became teardrops
And Mama's numbers.

*My mother used to play the "Numbers" and sometimes didn't have
paper to do her "workouts," so she used the Study Bible. I still have
the book.*

Created in September, 2006

Cilla Green

WE LIGHT THE CANDLES

"Let the light so shine before men, that they may see your good works and glorify your Father in Heaven... Matthew 5:16

We rejoice in the light
Of these candles tonight
That illuminates the lives created for us
Through God's love and grace and trust.
     We light the candles
Humbly, honoring family and friends of our past
Who built foundations of our lives to last
Knowing the struggles of the times they had
Keeping busy during good days and bad.

They guided our paths, teaching us lessons of life
Through patience, much love and some survival strife.
Keeping that foundation everlasting and strong
Letting us know this is where we belong
     We light the candles.
For Mamas who told us special stuff to survive
Molding us to live prayerful, more meaningful lives
And Daddies too, for just being there,
Whose "I meant what I said" was everywhere
     We light the candles
Even those we most needed and miss
Whose absences we longed for, was somewhat amiss

For our family and friends this very day
With whom we've come a long, long way
Thanking the Lord for those tender moments we share
When we needed someone to really care
     We light the candles
For our youth who have touched our tender heart
We thank you for being there from the start
Staying strong for us, making us proud
Standing up, above the crowd

The little ones who look into our eyes
Reflecting the candlelight with delightful surprise
For our newborn babies, celebrating their first Christmas light
We light the candles for them all tonight

We hope one day they will light a candle for us
As they remember that foundation built on love, faith and trust
That they will take it in their hands with tender loving care
Knowing that we will always be there, there, there
We light the candles.
To God be the Glory!

New Covenant United Church of Christ Candlelight Service,
December 28, 2008

STEP II   MEMBERS ONLY: ADDING DELICIOUS FLAVORS

Contributions of poetry and prose from members of New Covenant; expressions of memories of loved ones; joy in one's journey; a bit of art from Jean Jemison; all especially prepared with love. Here is an exciting addition of a college student's thoughts on the challenges and thoughts of life.

Isaiah 63:9
"In His love and mercy, He redeemed them"

MIA KAI SIMONNE MOODY... A JOURNEY

(A letter sent to New Covenant from her mother, Verona Moody)

December 15, 2007

Dear Family and Friends,

Season's Greetings, and best wishes for a healthy and peaceful New Year! This past year has been an exciting one for our beloved Mia Kai Simonne. Thank you all again for the many gifts and prayers that accompanied our loved one during her life-changing trip to Ghana, West Africa.

Mia spent the spring semester of 2007 at the University of Cape Coast, in Cape Coast, Ghana, where she truly grew up. She stated, "Ghana emancipated me. As I walked the dusty roads of the many villages I visited, Africa called to me. In the beautiful faces of the people I met, they openly embraced me, and said to me, 'Daughter, welcome home!'

"As I stood in the Atlantic Ocean, looking at the most magnificent blue sky, I silently gave thanks to the Lord for my safe arrival. I further thanked him for my parents and for my village of family and friends who have assisted in raising, supporting and loving me. I thanked him for the wonderful going- away party given by the extraordinary Justine Harris and attended by many of you. I took you all to Ghana with me.

"The ocean beckoned me further, and as I walked through the water, it became rougher. I felt pulled. The water swished around my ankles, angrily. I stood still, not wanting to forget one moment of this. In the stillness of the moment, a warm breeze embraced me, blowing through my braided hair. I looked down at the water now swilling at my feet, and I felt the pull of invisible hands at my ankles. In the wind gently blowing across my face I heard whispers, as if the ancestors were calling me! I was destined to be here! I felt I was born for this moment! I found out later that night that where I stood, many Africans threw themselves in the ocean rather than board the slave ships bound for this country. This experience resonated in my spirit, and influenced my semester Independent Study Project. It was titled, 'REMORY- The Blood Remembers; Psalm 9:12.'"

The Shallowhorn, Lee, and Clanton Families
Remember…OUR LOVED ONES

Each approached life with feet planted firmly on the ground, making them so special to us. Thus we continue to follow in their paths.

Compassionate, honest, going beyond the giving of self. Working long hours on the Treasury records. Seeking out persons who otherwise might never feel that they could be homeowners. Kind-hearted, forever giving a helpful hand with a smile.

Sense of being pleasant, concern for patients and their welfare. (Grace Shallowhorn).

Quiet, always on track, able to listen and give advice. (Geraldine Shallowhorn)

A smile that was his to give, that made you feel a sense of well-being. (Sidney Clanton).

"I'll do it. Where? What time? I'm on my way." (Bobby Lee) This sums up our loved ones.

"Well done"

"Servant of God"

"To God Be the Glory"

(Shallowhorn, Lee, and Clanton Families)

THE LOST SOUL

Where did you go?
No one seems to know.
You were here. You were there,
Huh, you were everywhere.
Things with you often went awry.
We wouldn't know when and we
Didn't know why.
But we were all left with broken
Family ties.

We whisper your name or pretend
You don't exist.
But the truth of the matter is,
Your name is on the list.
What did you struggle with? What did
You seek?
Did it make you less than a person or
Make you weak?

A flash in my head in the middle of
Night,
And there you were with this bright,
Radiant light.
Was this a message you wanted to
Send my way?
Was there something you wanted to say?
If so, then it's true: God forgives us Anyway!

(By Marilyn Gault)

THOUGHTS OF A JOURNEY

Oh! What a great joy this has been for my family and me since I began my journey with New Covenant UCC! The journey began many days ago and has stretched into many exciting years.

I have come to realize that whatever my service to this church has been, it was to please and honor God, not me.

There are many New Covenant members who have, perhaps unknowingly, had a profound influence on my Spiritual life. I thank you for this.

There are those who have passed into Eternity whom I have loved, admired and appreciated. Rest in peace.

I must thank Rev. Brown for his friendship, as well as insight and Spiritual guidance, as my Pastor, through the years.

Just to quote a few words from testimony: as I look back over my life and my journey with New Covenant, I can truly say, "I have been blessed."

(Maxine Bennett and Family)

FROM ANTHONY

I thank God for allowing me to realize
How He specialized
In having His Word internalized

In my mind, body and soul,
So there would no longer be a hole
Deep as the distance between the North and South Poles

He has created in me a new heart
So I would have a specific part
In His intricate art.

Making me look up in the darkness of night
Without worldly fright
Knowing my Lord and Savior is the light.

So whenever I get into a daze
Because of long, weary days
I always remember -- Jesus Saves!

(by Anthony Brown)

2 Timothy 2:15
"Study to shew thyself approved unto God, a workman that needeth not be ashamed, rightly divining the word of truth."

REMEMBERING AND HONORING

Mr. Charles Gayles, father of Dorothy Eaton, was an Instructor in the Bible Study class I attended. He also had all the beautiful windows installed in the Church.

Mr. Bill Michaels, one of the few Caucasian members of New Covenant, was a member of the Deacon Board. Every Saturday, he would be there to open the door to let me in to prepare the Altar cloths, when I served on the Deacon Board. Bill kept some of the Church records and knew where everything was in the building.

These two men and many others helped build the foundation of our New Covenant Church. I thank and remember them.

(From Eleanor Atkins)

One afternoon, at the August 2009 cookout, we sat around the table talking about our beloved members who had passed on, and had made such an impression on our Church. One person we discussed was Bro. Barnes, who was an active man, a jack-of-all-trades who could fix most anything. He used to cook a leg of lamb with lettuce flavored with the juices, for our Maundy Thursday Service. He loved to hunt and fish. Once, as the story goes, he was missing on a hunting trip for three hours. His companions thought he was hunting, but he was stuck in mud up to his hips. We remember those days, Bro. Barnes.

Another name we recalled was Mr. Guy Outlaw, husband of Pearl. Guy was involved in every aspect of Church activities. One time he organized a Retreat for members to Dunkirk Conference grounds. We slept in cabins, cooked our food, and had seminars concerning goals for the Church. What a fellowship that was! We remember you, Guy.

There were so many names, like Geraldine Shallowhorn,

who kept our financial books in order for so many years. Grace, Mel Coley who kept the Church fixed up, Doris, Louise, Mildred, Clara, Hattie, Nancy, Bessie, Gist, Carrie – and so many others that I regret not naming at this time. They will be remembered in our hearts.

(With love, from Priscilla, Helen, Jackie H., Veteran, Mrs. Moss and Geraldine.)

We are honoring Mrs. Cornelia Moss, who at age ninety-seven is our oldest member. We call her "Mother Moss," and old friends and family used to call her "Neel". She was born in Fayetteville, North Carolina, and raised in Americus, Georgia. When she was a little girl, Mother Moss would visit her maternal grandparents, who lived on the Indian Reservation there.

Her family moved to Buffalo, NY when she was thirteen years of age. They soon joined Lloyd's Memorial Church, where she always worked with the youth organizations. Mother Moss had the first Youth Usher Board and was a Deacon. Even today, she is involved with the Buffalo Youth, Young Adult Choral Association, after forty-two years of service and traveling all over the country.

Mrs. Cornelia Moss married Robert Moss in 1931, with whom she had eight children – six boys and two girls. She is proud that she "brought them up in the church." She said, "When I get there, they'd better be waiting for me!"

Thank you, Mother Moss, for being a faithful member of New Covenant UCC, matriarch of the Moss family and of our New Covenant UCC family, too.

The late Mrs. Annie Kimp, an avid reader, prolific writer, a New Covenent Church clerk and faithful long-time member, wrote these next three selections. She is the mother of Margaret English, who submitted these beautiful stories.

GOD'S DIVINE BOUQUET

Build Academy can be justly proud, because when God decided to create His bouquet, He looked down from His high heaven and chose choice flowers from our school family to enhance it. Flowers from this bouquet were chosen carefully, lovingly. They had to be of prime quality. He picked Robert Merritt, Mary Ellen White, and Jeffrey Marciana as buds to be placed in the center. For a rose just beginning to unfurl, He chose Byron Lawrence and Jeremy Lockwood.

He needed roses in full bloom, radiant, vibrant roses: Irma Dixon, Maxine Rukabeen, Jane Howard, Lonnie Hawkins, and Marge Rauh. Although His creation was wondrous to behold, for Him it was not complete. He was not satisfied. He thought, "I must have one more perfect flower. I wonder how my bouquet would look with an orchid among the roses. An orchid would add elegance and versatility." Again He looked down at our beloved Build Academy and chose Eula Pennington. Then He said, "My divine Bouquet is complete." How tenderly, how lovingly God must nurture His creation.

Although our lives have been saddened by the loss of our dear ones, just remember that someday we will have a chance to view this wondrous beauty, a bouquet created by God himself. I am sure that He has placed it in the center of His heaven and has labeled it, "God's Divine Bouquet".

"No man is an island, entire of itself. Each man's death diminishes me, for I am a part of mankind. Therefore send not for whom the bell tolls, it tolls for thee".

(Humbly submitted by Annie Kimp)

WE SHALL OVERCOME

"WE SHALL OVERCOME" is a song closely associated with our beloved Dr. Martin Luther King, Jr. Yes, we have overcome some of the racial barriers he lived and died for. For instance, we, as African-Americans, no longer have to go to the back of the bus in order to get a seat. In theaters, it is not compulsory to sit in balconies only. There are no signs designating colored and white facilities. We may go to any restaurant and be served. Great strides have been made in politics. African-Americans have been chosen as Mayors in such large cities as New York City (a first); Cleveland, Ohio; Seattle, Washington; Atlanta, Georgia; Detroit, Michigan; Charlotte, North Carolina; and in our nation's capital, Washington D.C. Unbelievably, an African-American was elected as governor of one of our southern states, Virginia.

When we remember that we, as Blacks, were restricted in our voting rights, we can say, "Yes, we have overcome." And we have, to a degree. In our own city of Buffalo, we have attained strategic jobs at City Hall: in the Common Council, we have George K. Arthur as President; James Pitts, former Majority Leader; David Collins, Archie Amos, and Clifford Bell. We have Roger Blackwell and William Robinson in County government. We must not forget Supreme Court Justice, Samuel Green, who is the only Black member of the Supreme Court in Buffalo. On the Board of Education there are prominent Black members; the former principal of Build Academy, Mrs. Johnny Mayo, now holds an important position in education at City Hall.

Yet, there is still discrimination, there is still bigotry existing. In housing, certainly, in employment and in health care. We all know that prisoners are not treated equally when they stand before a judge, because most of the Blacks are too poor to pay the exorbitant fee for a reputable lawyer. These are only a few of the ways that we, as African-Americans, are unequal, yet these are the very issues for which Dr. Martin Luther King, Jr. gave his life.

"WE SHALL OVERCOME, WE SHALL OVERCOME

SOMEDAY…WE SHALL ALL BE FREE. WE SHALL BE FREE SOMEDAY." You, my friends, may ask, "When? When will all this happen?"

The answer, my friends, is written in the wind. The answer is written in the wind.

(Written by Annie Vernel Kimp
January 1990)

BELIEVE

BELIEVE in Faith and Prayers
      and
Prayers and Angels that watch over us

BELIEVE in New Days
      that
Bring New Beginnings

BELIEVE in Amazing Grace
      and
Miracles that happen
Where we least expect to find them

BELIEVE in God
Who wants only the
Best and brightest for you
      Always

(By Eleanor Atkins)

This section consists of essays and poetry that are fervent expressions of Patrick's views of life and its challenges. Patrick is a student at the University of Buffalo, the son of Barbara Davis, and a member of New Covenant United Church of Christ.

GOOD MORNING

Wake up! It is you whom I instruct to awaken and open your eyes to this disaster of what we call the world. Why are we so naïve in our misunderstandings of the reasons why things happen in our lives? In an alarming number of cases, we are the ones who cause our own pain and regret. It is we who tend to view so many things as innocuous; but it gnaws on our innocent perceptions and it is time for us to mature.

It is our dreams that we tend to abjure, as we search for a suitable present solution to our struggles and pains in this world full of lust and desire. But we must abstain from this, and remember that we are what we make ourselves. We need not the entire overflowing plate, with money and material nourishment. We must learn to consume abstemious "meals", teach our bodies and minds not to desire such hefty unreachable feats.

Look out your window: don't glance, don't glare, don't peek... I ask of you to stare deep down into the abyss of lies that are told to us young people. See what drugs, violence and heartbreak are doing to us and our families and every single living person on this planet. You don't see you it, do you? You don't see the seventeen-year-old boy sitting in his living room, prepping a heroin-filled syringe. It makes me sick to my stomach; it has left an acidulous taste in my mouth.

What happened to us young people? What has adulterated our minds to make us believe that guns will solve all problems, and that killing one of our brethren is okay? What the hell gives people the idea that killing someone will aggrandize oneself? That makes you a murderer, not a street soldier. It makes you a loser and a sellout; and most of all it makes you a disgrace to all that we human beings have accomplished – Life.

Maybe what I've said in this poetry aggravates some, but it is I who could care less. I speak what is from the heart; I speak what mine eyes have seen throughout my twenty-one years of life. They bleed the tears of sorrow as I rain pity upon the individuals that feel as though there is no way to achieve or to grow. But I say this to you: if you are alive, you have time to change. If you have legs, a wheelchair, crutches, cane, prosthetic legs or anything, you can take steps to a better future.

I refuse to believe that PEACE has become an anachronistic term. I refuse to believe that the streets are the only place to turn for acceptance, family, money and other items. I refuse to believe that the crescendo of pain that resides in our hearts will continue to be. This is real talk, coming from a young black man grown up in a generation of artificial hip-hop full of false messages, falling governments, war and continuing hate.

Maybe the world I wish to awaken into is a fantasy; perhaps I should give encomium to the time I live in. The science of my mind and maturity is esoteric to God and to me. I wish upon the stars and ask that one day, I will awaken into the reality of my fantasy world – and then, that I will have a "Good Morning…"

"DNA-97"

The wind outlines my face
As I sail across the oceans
Salty breeze cools my moist skin
The sunshine glistens on the waves
The wind expands the sail
Noise of the ruffling and wrinkling
Echoes within my ear canal
Mist from the waves
Pleasantly stings my eyes
I lean over the bow of the boat
And allow the water to flow between my fingers
It is as warm as the skin
That resides on my back
Which the sun has kissed with its heat waves
Dolphins approach this entity that is myself
This image is one that will never be forgotten
Oh, how life seems to become
An intricate bevy of fantasies
All seems so well and fruitful
Direction had no relevancy in my life
Yet I sail towards the
Bermuda Triangle
The mast begins to dematerialize
Imitating the mist that floats
So freely in every direction
I know my end is near
I will not fret
I will not fear
I will not make a wish
It is my destiny
I stand against the waves and wind
I raise my arms from my sides
I lift my head to the sun
I slowly close my eyes
My chest high and open
I embrace what will become of me

I begin to dematerialize as the wood around me
I fade into the atmosphere of the Earth
For I am not deceased
I have become a part of you
It is in you that I will live forever.

(By Patrick D. Crosby)

GOOD NIGHT

Dear Diary:

It is late. From where I reside, 'tis dark in the skies; but elsewhere in the world many are experiencing day. Yet here, here in my life, my surroundings, my world, this does not exist. I say this not as a pessimist, but as an individual who refuses to live his life with his eyes and mind closed. I see, I hear, I feel the world coming to an end; I fear it is not the physical planet, but worlds residing within the minds of its inhabitants.

I am the connoisseur of nothing. I do not claim to be the reincarnation of Nostradamus; I am no psychic. I claim none of this – but I do claim to pay attention. I look at many associates and shake my head in pity. Society has desiccated their moist minds, which now thirst for a potent ephemeral replacement. Do people not see that they need more than this? Wake up, world, please! But most feel it is too late.

In this mind of mine, if there is a pulse that enlivens your body, if there is a brain inside the protective casing of the skull, if you have a dream, it will never be too late. Abdication of one's life does not have to occur if you will not allow it. I do not understand what has happened to the world, after the many years of humanity's existence. I am not a history major; but as I am alive, I have come to realize that I am history.

Think: individuals risked their lives for freedom, yet we murder one another and strip it away along with life. My ancestors risked their lives to learn to read, write, and educate themselves; yet today, the desire to stay in school dies every hour. Other ancestors and relatives have been massacred because of their religious beliefs, who in many cases did not deny affiliation; today we deny the simple idea of where we came from.

We've given up words to pick up a gun; abandoned books to pick up dice; sacrificed our children to produce more; deserted love and developed abuse; cast off morals and reverted back to savage ways. Why is it that guns can't fire butterflies? Why can't syringes contain holy water? Why can't books be read instead of used as toilet paper soiled with digested lies, false beliefs, and false reality?

Hmm… happy endings: in this world there is no such thing. But a happy ending is desired more than the urge to reach heaven, or any other afterlife that is pleasant and welcoming. War remains around the world. It is not only in our streets, our schools, and our homes, but also in ourselves. One wants to succeed, but refuses to apply oneself. One wants marriage, but refuses to treat one's significant other properly.

We refuse to recognize that one Good Evening, but listen to the lies that society tells us. I would advise them to silence themselves and listen to the world around them, to open their eyes and witness the catastrophes occurring every minute of every day. I'd ask them to put out their hands and feel the tears running down the face of widows, now-fatherless children, mothers and fathers who lost one of their prized possessions. Feel the screams of the pain rumble in your heart.

It is time for me to rest my eyes, for I have seen enough damage in this day. But tomorrow may be a Good Morning. I say to you, "Good Night."

(By Patrick D. Crosby)

WHAT'S HAPPENING: BUS DRIVER #3

Renaldo Rodriguez loved to drive, especially big cars or trucks. When his parents brought him to Buffalo, New York, fifty years ago, in search of a better life, and to be closer to relatives, he was a skinny, scared, Spanish teenager.

Now, in 1999, Mr. Rodriguez has been married to Marta for thirty-five years. They have four children, ages ten, fifteen, twenty, and twenty-three. Two are in college and the other two are in Catholic Schools. "Praise the Lord, we got good kids," says Marta, when asked about her family.

Renaldo has kept his 185-pound body in good shape. He speaks English fluently, but with a heavy accent – which is probably the reason he has west-side routes most of the time. Marta, a second-grade ESL Teacher at a neighborhood school, loves the dimples in his cheeks, especially when he smiles and shows (his own) white teeth; loves his bushy eyebrows that make him look comical; but she says he needs to trim his moustache down and let his close-cropped salt-and-pepper hair grow out, just a tad.

Mr. Renaldo Rodriguez was on the last leg of his weekend shift. It was a cool, clear, Saturday evening, in September. He always felt anxious on these nights.

"Gotta find another route or another job. Just five more years to go."

He thought of Al and Charles, who were going to celebrate their retirement next Friday, at a Fish Fry. "Why? I don't know," he reflected. "Just as well. The boys don't want nothing too special."

Mr. Rodriguez pulled the long bus to the corner of Porter and Mariner Streets, waiting for six o'clock. Several people got on. Three teenage girls laughed and giggled about a young boy they had just met. One wore huge, round, gold earrings, a scarf tied around her ponytail and a long pinkish sweater. The other two were very colorful, even this late in September.

His route continued along the west-side streets. He stopped to pick up his varied passengers, as the sun set quickly and darkness emerged, showing off that bright, ominous full moon. Mr. Rodriguez enjoyed this part of his job… all the colorful characters, young and old, talkative and quiet ones too.

The black-hooded young man came behind the odd hippie-looking couple. He fumbled for change, but pulled out a bus pass. The picture looked like him, about twenty, light brown skin, dark hair: maybe Hispanic, maybe mixed with something.

Mr. Rodriguez became nervous and sweat beaded on his forehead. It felt like *déjà vû*: he remembered when another hooded young man, whom he befriended, fumbled for change twenty years ago, almost to the day.

He had dark brown hair, sparkling eyes, and a polite smile, as he told Mr. Rodriguez that his girlfriend was having a baby any day now.

"It's a boy! His name will be Cortez, like mine."

At this point, the young man looked sad.

"What's the matter?" Mr. Rodriguez asked him.

" I need a job right now, so we can get married and keep the baby."

The burnished St. Christopher medal shone against his black clothing.

The bus stopped at Maryland and Wadsworth Street. As an old lady and her grandson boarded the bus, Mr. Rodriguez reached into his wallet and handed the young man a twenty-dollar bill.

The young man, named Cortez, pulled his hoodie over his

head and took a silver pistol from his pocket. The glare of the gun and the spirit of his medal made this moment feel so surreal.

"Oh, my God!" the old lady prayed softly.

"Sit down, old lady, and shut up!" shouted young Cortez. " I want all your money. No credit cards; just money! Okay, the rest of you, get your money out!"

He moved fast up the aisle, taking money from everyone, even the old lady's grandson's dollar, which he gave tearfully.

Mr. Rodriguez was startled. His hands trembled as he tried to push the panic button and put the bus into gear. The hooded robber jumped out of the rear door and ran. Terrified, Mr. Rodriguez pushed the gear in reverse. He bumped against something as he finally put the bus in the right gear and sped off. Several blocks later, he called the police from the bus phone.

He was shaken and scared like the ten passengers; some fled before the police could get there. Anger and fear were so deep, he wanted to scream and cry out loud.

"Well, it seems to be happening again," he said to himself.

When the hooded young man uncovered his head and smiled, Mr. Rodriguez saw the similarities. Before Mr. Rodriguez could see that the silver object the young man pulled out of his bag was just a silver pen, he had pushed the emergency button.

"So where are you going, young man?" he asked, with some hesitation.

"I'm going to my first Christian Poetry Slam at the University. I hope I'm not too late. I had to work overtime today. I'm a freshman at UB. My poetry is getting much better than when I first started two years ago. I'm working on something new. It's called 'What's Happening, Lord?' Wanna hear it?"

Before he could begin, the police sirens and lights came swirling, guns drawn as they entered the bus.

The Lieutenant asked, "What's happening? You okay?"

Mr. Rodriguez replied, quickly stuttering, "Yes-s-s, Sir. I must have pressed the button by mistake."

The Officer snarled and cussed, then thumped the door as he left.

The young man looked at Mr. Rodriguez with shared disgust, shook his head as he took off his jacket.

Mr. Rodriguez saw the glitter of something around the young man's shirt.

"Where did you get that from?"

"THANKS for asking," the young man said, emphasizing *thanks*. "It belonged to my Papi."

"Where is your Dad now?"

"Oh, he was killed in a bus accident before I was born," he answered, with sadness and irony in his voice. "So – you wanna hear some of my poem NOW?"

"Okay," Mr. Rodriguez said, with a lump in his throat.

"What's happening when you think I'm somebody I'm not?
What's happening when fear governs our lives?
*What's happening when trust is gone…*Hey, here's my stop.
I'll read some more the next time… *adiós*."

Mr. Rodriguez felt a twinge of regret in his heart, but he remembered the last time he embraced and trusted a hooded stranger on a night run. Then, he prayed that the robber would be caught and jailed. This time, he prayed for mercy.

STEP III   A TASTE OF SOUL: STIR CAREFULLY UNTIL BLENDED

A celebration of Black lives from way back in the day until now. Some poems were recited during Black History Month at New Covenant United Church of Christ. The two short stories are based on historical events, but fictionalized.

2 Corinthians 12:9
"My Grace is sufficient for you, for my power is made perfect in weakness."

FROM THE ICEMAN TO OBAMA

*"Iceman, Iceman, coming round; if you need some ice, come on
down.
Don't you young 'uns forget to empty the water trays for yo' mama!"*

The Iceman who cooled our summers with chips of ice
He warmed our hearts and was oh, so nice.
*Junkman. Junkman, gimme yo' old rags and newspaper and stuff, if
yo' got some;
Hurry, hurry up so I can get done."*

*"Hey, Miss Green, got some watermelon and cabbage; hope these
sweet potatoes will do.
And fo' that sweet young lady next do', got some green tomatoes
too."*

*"Aunty Mae, Aunty Mae, this Milkman's leaving you some cold, cold
milk with cream on top.
Gotta go this time; cain't even stop."*

*"Hurry, hurry ,ladies, y'all put yo' man's stuff away for another day;
'Cause that Welfare man is on his way.
Hurry... hurry, y'all."*

The Insurance man said, *"Ella, Got a special Going Home package
for ya at 50 cents a week.
I know you will like it. It's just what you seek."* (And we paid).

The Number man came by every day;
sometimes to give us a day's pay.
More likely, we gave our money away, a dime at a time.

The Jack store man gave me dreams of being a mathematician or
more,
Checking that notebook when he added extras at his grocery store.

The Max Liquor store man inspired us to be anybody we could,

As we devoured Johnny Walker Red, Old Granddad, and
Thunderbird.

Here comes the Preacher man, eating Ma's fried chicken, while
preaching the Word
telling us to tithe all our money on the third.

The Process man came smoothly too;
Doo-wapping on the corners, singing "There Goes my Baby,"
while we sang, "Maybe, Maybe, Maybe".

Jimmy Lyons at the Dellwood Ballroom, The Hadji Temple and the
Y's
gave us background music of our lives.

Then came the fine young men called the Phila Phala Phis,
who brought all of us young ladies to our knees.

The Matadors, who couldn't be beat,
Were the baddest young men on any street.

The Black Panthers cut their hair and let it grow,
So we wouldn't be Colored or Negroes anymo'.

The X man emerged and changed his name,
Giving us enough pride to do the same.

Along came Martin, the dreamer, it seems;
"Let us slay him," they said. "See what becomes of his dreams."

I probably missed some men you know,
but just two more before I go.

Out of the ashes, he stealthily came –
Barack Obama,
With the funny name,
Knowing he could cope;

Giving us the Audacity of Hope.

And then there's the Man called many names, who
Created all these men from the Iceman to Obama.

Priscilla Y. Hill
June 14, 2008

SOLDIERS OF COLOR

From the Revolutionary War,
Our soldiers of color were
Fighting in the battlefields
Fighting for freedom
For the colonists, the Union, the Korean,
The English, the French, the Polish
The Vietnamese, the Afghans, the Kuwaitis;
And now Iraq,
As they raised that flag high in the sky
And sang the National Anthem.

They were the first off the boat.
They were the first to fight,
The first to die;
They were the last in line,
The last to be honored
For the bravery we all knew they had
As they raised that flag high in the *sky*
And sang the National Anthem.

No ticker-tape parades for them:
The 369th, the Triple Nickels,
The Tuskegee Airmen, the Infantry,
The Quartermasters…
And the "Red Ball Express,"
Who should have been first
In the parade, like they were in war
As they raised the flag high in the sky
And sang the National Anthem.

Some came home,
Came home to their black folks
Who were so proud of them
As they stood tall in their fine uniforms.
We knew what they did,
Fighting all those wars

On all those battlefields.
But the biggest battlefield was called
The Homefront.
Battling discrimination…
Can't get no jobs.
Battling racism…
Can't live where they want.
Battling that mental turmoil
Deep inside their guts…
Struggling to be somebody
As they raised the flag high in the sky
And sang the National Anthem.

So for you, Black soldiers,
We give you reverence in our world.
We honor you with medals of the heart,
We give thanks to you with our words,
Because you <u>had</u> to be brave,
You <u>had</u> to be strong
Fighting all those battles…for <u>us</u>
As you raise the flag high in the sky
And sing loudly, 'We Shall Overcome."

December 16, 2005

MARTIN LUTHER KING: TIME FOR CHANGE

They knew it was time for change
When they talked 'bout that man. "What's his name?
He sure can preach," they said.

Some of them called him a troublemaker,
Trying to change white man's laws
That couldn't be changed,
'Cause some of them didn't want no trouble.

Some of them called him an arrogant Preacher man,
Preaching 'bout non-violence all the time
From a skinny Indian man named Gandhi;
And 'bout loving one another, whoever you are,
From a Savior named Jesus.
You see, some of them had lost all hope.

Some of them complained that the mountain he preached about
Was just too high; and the valley was way too low
To get to the other side.

Most of them knew he was coming
But wouldn't be there long.
They felt it in their hearts
As he marched them by the thousands
Down mean city streets
As he brought them together, walking as one
Boycotting the busses in Montgomery
And beginning a Civil Rights Movement.

They knew he wouldn't be there long
When he told them" We Shall Overcome;"
As he walked them into the voting booths to have their say,
As people died for a dream in buses, cars, streets and even churches.

They knew he wouldn't be there long

As they strutted into Mississippi Colleges and Alabama schools
While he received the Nobel Peace Prize,
And sat with Presidents and even the Pope…
It wouldn't be long.

They knew he wouldn't be there long
When he told them' bout going to the mountaintop,
As they rioted and looted in the streets
Where they once marched in peace.

They knew it wouldn't be long
When he was stabbed by Izola,
Jailed in Birmingham,
Stoned in Chicago;
And it wasn't long before hate
Killed this man of peace, in Memphis.

Martin Luther King. Jr.. he didn't stay long.
But he gave them, and us, dreams of hope, dreams of peace,
And dreams of equality.

January 2004
Priscilla Y. Parker-Hill

HILL HOUSE

CHAPTER ONE

Superintendent Davis read the headlines to Mrs. Stodlemier.

"NEWS FLASH...DRAFT RIOTS IN FIVE POINTS"

"As Superintendent of Hill House, I must warn you of trouble that is to come. You'll have to be prepared to leave soon," he told her as they stood on the white-railed front porch.

"What's going on, Mr. Davis?" Mrs. Stodlemier asked nervously, clasping her hands and biting her lips.

"President Lincoln signed the Conscription Act to bolster the Union Forces. Several Draft offices have been set up in Manhattan. They have lottery wheels to assign men to join the Union Forces; except if you can pay $300, you don't have to go. The Irish, who live in the Five Points neighborhood near us, are bitter. Recently they have been looting and burning the Draft Offices. They even lynched several black men. The paper quoted an Irish man, saying, "I will not be killed fo' no colored people."

Mrs. Stodlemier was the headmistress of the Colored Children's Asylum called Hill House. It was a four-story home on the corner of Fifth Avenue, from 43rd to 44th Streets. It opened in 1837, beautifully surrounded by huge maple trees. Hill House was a place for colored orphans who had lost their parents, or parents who lost them. Mrs. Stodlemier's body was large like her heart, whose bosom held and loved hundreds of children, mostly colored, but some white ones too. They loved her whiskers on her chin and smile that warmed their hearts. She was their mom, but they called her Miss Stoddie

.

"I knew something was wrong when I got a visit from Mr. Murphy," she said to Mr. Davis.

"Mrs. Stodlemier," Mr. Murphy stammered, when he came to deliver groceries one day last month. "I'm an old man who don't want no trouble. You been getting your provisions from me for a long time. I thank you. But I can't be a man and let bad things happen to children, 'specially God's children. Well, Ma'am, I heard 'em talkin' and getting drunk. So you be careful and get them children out of here."

"I knew there was trouble, but I thought he was exaggerating a bit."

"No, he was not. He probably didn't tell you *enough*," said Mr. Davis, as he walked down the porch steps. "Be careful, and think about what he said."

Mrs. Stodlemier's face burned crimson. She had had a bad feeling for some time, ever since Mr. Tyler, that red-headed usurper of people's properties, asked her to sell the Orphanage to him.

"You kindly sell me this property; I will give you a fair price. I do need to extend my property," he told her.

She cringed, but replied," I've been here for twenty-six years or more, taking care of hundreds of children over those years. Where are we going to go, Mr. Tyler?"

Seeing the evilness creeping over Mr. Tyler's face, Mrs. Stodlemier added, "Just give me some time to discuss it with the Board. Hopefully, that would give me a few more months to decide what to do."

She thought to herself, *"It has been some long, tough years. I am getting older. The children are getting worse. I had to send a few of them to another place last year."*

"Well, I'll see," said Mr. Tyler, ending this frightening conversation.

CHAPTER TWO

Ophelia was about six or seven, ginger-colored with lollipop lips, and Aida's baby sister. She smelled something funny that made her cough, which she did often because she was fragile and small for her age. They never knew her birthday, but Miss Stoddie gave her June 5th, in the afternoon. Aida felt her fidgeting and heard her coughing.

Aida was twelve, the oldest of the thirty-six children, and everybody loved her. She was tall for her age, strong, with dark cocoa-brown skin and the whitest teeth. She would tell the children she chewed on a special bark that tasted like dried apples. Aida and Ophelia had been living at Hill House for the last two years. She hoped this would be the last home for them.

Aida was always attentive; always smelling, feeling and listening. That night Aida was the first to smell the smoke, then someone's scream pervaded the rooms, startling everyone.

As Mrs. Stodlemier dozed in the overstuffed chair, planning their escape, her head rolled back and a loud snore sneaked out of her mouth, frightening her. "Oh my God, I fell asleep!" she cried. She heard the shrill scream and knew it was time.

Mrs. Stodlemier calmed the children with her soft-pitched, yet strong voice. From the smallest child (who was two years old) to the oldest, they trusted her. They quieted nervously, because they had practiced this emergency at least once a week for the past two years. There was a sign on the walls: WHAT TO DO IN CASE OF A FIRE.

Miss Stoddie, Aida, and Miss Dengu, their cook and helper, gathered the children into the dining room.

"Okay, now. Quiet and listen. Pick up your bundles and walk to the basement. Girls, you know what to do." They picked up prepared bundles for each one as they meandered towards the basement door.

The spirited flames whipped up the sides of the old, rugged, wood-frame house that had stood there for seventeen years. The reddish-orange color of destruction licked the walls, the stairs, ceilings, cracked the windowpanes, spurring billows of smoke through all the crevices, painting it all with grunge, grime and death, sucking out all the life.

CHAPTER THREE

In the Five Points area of Manhattan lived a diversified, yet separated, ethnic mixture. The largest group was the Irish, then the Jewish, German, Italian, Chinese and Colored. This was the most notorious slum. Here, stolen elections were common, because jobs were few for the unskilled. There was fighting between the Irish and other groups over these few jobs, especially when the coloreds came north. Hundreds of colored men were lynched. Brothels and saloons were plentiful. There was drunkenness and disease living in overcrowded tenements and filthy streets, where they say tap-dancing was first performed in the streets.

The drunken men from the Four Corners did not have enough of fighting and killing each other. One night, after hours of drinking rum and gruel, they emerged with sticks, stones and fists to fight once more. The young Irish boy, who hated all of this, but was scared not to be a man, vomited all over some of the men standing next to him. This kind of quieted some of the men, but angered others.

The clouds hung low and dark, threatening to burst open on the heat of all this hatred. But they waited too.

The old man with the wrinkled face and scowl saw them hesitate. He shouted, "Why the hell we fighting each other? Let's get the ones that started all this. Burn the Darkies down in that old

house. They may be young 'uns, but they gonna grow up one day."
The two oil drums sat there ominously, waiting for the hatred to
intensify, waiting like soldiers, ready to kill, ready to die.

The strong young men hoisted the huge barrels filled with
oil, stumbling, half-running on overzealous adrenalin, leading the
march to the Colored Orphanage.

"Hey, y'all, wait a minute!" yelled one of the men. "Lets git
some of the stuff they's got, afo' we burn 'em down. What about
that, huh?"

The crowd of about one hundred men burst through the door.
They searched for valuables. They looted the four-story building,
even carried off baby clothes, toys, or anything near them.
One of the men shouted, "Okay, that's it. If'n ya ain't got
what you want, too bad! Lets git ta burnin'!"

They rolled the oil drums towards the house, lifting them to
the porch, rolling them through the smashed doors. Torches were
thrown on all sides of the house. Men were running, shouting,
screaming, "Where them chillen' at?" However, the blazing glow of
the fire distracted them for the moment.

CHAPTER FOUR

All thirty-six children, Miss Dengu, and Miss Stoddie
headed towards the huge door in the basement. They walked close
to the floor, hunched over, carrying the younger children through
the tunnel, which was four feet high by six feet wide. This was an
escape slave route that was built with the house. It curved about a
hundred yards behind the house towards the stream.

Sounds of crying and whimpering permeated the tunnel, as
the children and Miss Stoddie carefully walked to the old wooden
door at the end. Smoke crept stealthily closer to them, as Miss
Stoddie made sure no one stopped or slowed down. It was getting

hotter too. "Maybe we didn't close the door tight enough?" she thought.

Suddenly the line stopped. Aida cried out, "The door...the door is stuck! We can't get out!" as panic gripped her.

"Open up!" shouted Miss Stoddie, as she burst through the children, who knew she was coming and got out of her way. With the force of all her body and life, she ran and banged the door. It only nudged a little bit. She ran back and forth, banging the door with her body, smelling the oil-soaked smoke approaching. "Oh, Lord, help us," she prayed silently. With the last strength she had, Miss Stoddie's body pressed on the door as it fell, splintered, to the floor. She said, "Thank you, Lord, for opening this door, and for the pain in my shoulder."

It was still dark. except for the bright glow of Hill House burning. As the Orphanage blazed, the clouds burst open as if they had waited long enough. The children, with Aida, Miss Stoddie and Miss Dengu, Mr. Davis, the Superintendent, and several people he asked to help were silhouetted in the fire's light and the smoke of cinders wet from the rain.

"What a blessing and a wonderful surprise, to realize we were not alone! Thank you all," Miss Stoddie said, and hugged each one.

Miss Stoddie had prepared for this journey ever since she opened the Colored Children's Asylum, with her sister Harriett, twenty-two years ago. She had friends in Connecticut, Massachusetts, and Vermont who were preparing to welcome them.

Everyone except Mr. Davis and his friends crossed the stream, where they were startled to see a large wagon awaiting them. The driver was none other than the red-headed man who had tried to frighten Mrs. Stodlemeir into selling him the Orphanage!

"I knowed y'all needed some transport, so here I am. Come on. Git in. Quick now!" said Mr. Tyler.

PASSING THE TORCH

"Empty and dark shall I raise my lantern" [1]

We Torch Bearers, dreamers of dreams, lovers of life
Illuminating the darkness
Letting the world know where we've been
Firing up the torch that lights the way
For all the world to see
Seeking truths in these dreams.

Torch Bearers
Carrying the light of wisdom
In the autumn of our lives,
To generations we've created
Who simmer and wait their time
To grasp the torch,
Anticipating a good run
Anxious to know where we come from
And where they need to go.

Torch Bearers
Who accepted the chosen challenge?
Knowing the burden was heaviest
When we had to fight
To keep the flame from flickering.
Sometimes we had to light a fire
Under somebody
To awaken the sleeping giants
While burning bright this torch of light
That gave us stamina,
Persistence, pride, faith and hope.

"In the darkest hour of our lives
Look for the Midnight Specialist" [2]
Who lit the way with the North Star.

Then we passed the Torch

To the next generation of Torch Bearers
Where we became colored
Where we carried the torch
For Mary B. Talbert, W.E.B. Dubois,
And so many others.

They too, passed it on
To the freedom fighters of the 60s
Who died while holding the light

With strong, bold arms
Keeping the flame everlasting.

We've had a long, hard journey
Passing the torch, keeping it lit
Overcoming hurdles, jump-shots
And blind-sided tackles
Keeping us forever watchful
In this arena of life.

But this torch
Inspires the fire within us
Safeguards the flame outside us
For generations to come.

Let us pass it on…

For Rev. Will J. Brown's class reunion, April 24, 2004

[1,2] Quotes from "The Prophet," by Kahlil Gibran

EDMONIA'S CLEOPATRA

There you stand... six feet high,
My Cleopatra... white, smooth, Italian marble
Shaped with Edmonia's hands.

Your head turned slightly, looking down on me.
A ghastly stare into nothingness,
Brought gasps from opened mouths.
The asp rests startling on your breasts,
As the folds of your gown succinctly
Caress your body.

You were a headstone for a grand stallion
At a racetrack,
A grotesquely painted statue, guarding
The entrance to a tavern.
You were a lost masterpiece, waiting to be found.

Standing tall among the warehouse debris.
A stranger with an inquisitive eye
Focused on you, in the midst of all this chaos,
Wondering what he had found...
Wondering if the world was ready for you.

As he touched you tenderly,
Stroking away layers of years,
Your creator silently emerged,
Screaming to be free... again

Now you sit elegantly
At the Smithsonian,
In a shadowed room
For all the world to see.

This poem is about Edmonia Lewis, who was part African and part Oneida
(?) Indian. She attended Oberlin College for a brief time. Later she went
to France to pursue her career as a sculptor, where she found the marble to

work with and financial support.   The sculpture of Cleopatra was found in 1970, refurbished, and now sits in the Smithsonian Museum in Washington D.C.

Priscilla Y. Hill

October 2002

WHO ARE YOU, MARY B. TALBERT?

Mary Talbert, Mary Talbert…
Were you the Talbert Mall
whose name was changed to
Frederick Douglas Towers,
because no one knew
you were a black woman?

Are you the Talbert Hall
on the grounds of U.B.
where no one knows your name,
as they saunter in and out
of your doors?

Mary Talbert,
Did you fight against the
lynching of our colored people
and for the rights,
of colored women
to vote and be recognized?

Did you stage a protest during
the Pan-American Exposition in Buffalo,
because of the degradation of Negroes,
at the Colored Exhibition, in the Midway?

Does your oak dining-room table
still stand tall, from the strength
of Frederick Douglas and W.E.B. Dubois
planning the foundation
of the Niagara movement?

Mary Talbert,
Did you help advance the rights
of people of color,
people who still don't
know who you are?

Mary Talbert, Mary Talbert...
Who are you?
Where are you?

Written by Priscilla Hill, 5/2003

Presented at the Mary B. Talbert
Civic & Cultural Club Banquet,
April 22, 2006

1866-1923

RISING FROM THE ASHES

The sumptuous smells of red beans and rice
Of shrimp, of jambalaya, of fried catfish,
Hot Jazz and moody Blues on sultry nights.
And some places called Parishes.
People of many hues whose voices mix
Delicately in choirs of Baptist churches.
All blended over hundreds of years,
Quickly quieted in August, 2005
By Nature's wrath, called Katrina.

A new kind of devastation…
Help was slow in coming
From unseen faces.
Soon, though, it came from many places.
And through all of this chaos
Emerged a spirit of human kindness,
From a man with a hotel to spare,
From a woman with too many houses,
From the world of Entertainment,
From people within our nation
And all over the world.

We marvel at the inner strength of people
From Alabama, Mississippi and Louisiana;
At their resolve to never give up;
The determination to keep their dreams alive,
For families staying together.
We are amazed at their faith, their hope
That will bring about their renewal.

Images are still haunting
As people stand in solidarity,
Creating new lives in new places.
In temporary homes, people forge
Strong bonds; and many will stay.

Others will return for the reconstruction
And the restoration.

Now it's time to rise again through faith,
Through hope from healing.
Remembrances shared and passed on
Of loved ones who did not survive.
Through memories of the scents of their
Neighborhoods; of stories told that still inspire,

Creating and spreading that special coastal culture,
Wherever you call home…
And once again you will rise, rise, rise
From the ashes.

December 2005

FAR FROM THE DRUMS

We have come far from the drums of Africa
To the Griots, telling stories and spreading the word.
Far from the Negro spirituals sending hidden messages,
From the Preachers sermonizing 'bout the conductor that was
coming.
We sang, we beat those drums, we danced:
Masta thought we was happy.
But we were stirring slowly the stew called freedom.

Mary Terrell knew it and educated the world about it.
Ida B. Wells wrote about the strange fruit
Swinging in the southern trees.
Mary B. Talbert came to the table, creating
A movement called Niagara.
Harriet Tubman and Frances Harper were convinced
By improving family life and developing strength of character
We could stir this stew called freedom.

They had seen the empty pot waiting to be tended.
They filled it with the Spirit of life,
Added spices to give it character,
A bit of salt and sugar for conflict.
They needed God's blessings, though, to give it substance,
And prayers to meld the flavors together.

These uncrowned Queens served it hot,
Warming our hearts and strengthening our minds,
Making us long for more –
More of this stew called freedom.
Thus, one by one, our race is lifted... and filled

Written for Black History Month in February, 2002

Priscilla Y. Parker

A JOURNEY TO THE TEMPLE

The women came fully dressed in their sleek, Victorian couturier dresses, with plumed hats and parasols. They snickered, laughed, huddling together, amazed at this Buffalo city of twinkling lights. Their escorts, in derby hats, waistcoats, and pocket watch chains, gawked at the blackness of the real Africans, who had to wear symbols of their oppression: the bones in the nose, spears in the fists, and the skimpy animal skins, at the living African Village, on the Midway, at the World's Fair Pan-American Exposition, in America, 1901.

I used to love sitting in Mrs. Talbert's parlor of overstuffed chairs, accented by shiny mahogany wood, with puffy pillows, all in shades of wine and mauve, with touches of dark blue. Soft, sinuous smells of lavender and spices from the kitchen lingered everywhere. The downstairs rooms were filled with portraits of Negroes, Native Indians, and a few white people, too. There I listened to the stories of Ida B. Wells and Harriett Tubman; and also about the lynchings in the South and North. They told me memorable stories about the freed slaves and those who, like the Talberts, became the pillars of the colored and white communities.

Mrs. Mary B. Talbert was an upper-class, well-to-do colored woman whom I loved and respected. She was a tall, heavy-set woman, full of pride, like her African/Oneida father. Her dark hair was always piled upon her head, accenting her cinnamon-colored skin, smooth as silk, like her Indian mother's. Mrs. Talbert was the first president of the Buffalo Colored Women's Club. Women like Francis Young and Mrs. Charles Green wrote articles in newspapers like the *Courier* and the *Gazette*, which had the courage to print them, to protest the degradation of Negro people and the exclusion of Negroes on the Board of Directors of the Expo.

Mrs. Talbert's husband was a businessman. Some of his clients were financially well-off; but he also helped those who could only give him a chicken for the pot or a sumptuous Sunday dinner, or even do some designated chores around his property.

Soon their home became the meeting place for prominent Negro men like Frederick Douglas, W.E.B. Dubois, and Rev. Jesse Nash, pastor of the Michigan Street Baptist Church. These men later created the Niagara Movement.

At twenty-two years of age, a graduate of Oberlin College, in Ohio, I, Hilda Watt, became the first of my large family (three sisters and four brothers) to complete any education above the sixth grade. My family – momma, daddy and grandmother – lived in a small country town called Greenwood, Ohio. They were delighted when I chose to study at Oberlin, a small, select, liberal arts college that accepted colored girls. Still, they were a little wary of me going alone. Aunt Melinda warned me that I had too big a butt for a small gal, and my milk-chocolate coloring was sure to entice a lot of men.

"Someplace lek thet could cause ya lots o' trouble, my Hillie," said Momma, many times. But the excitement of being "away from home" was a long-thought-out journey, even in the fall of 1897.

My Aunt Melinda talked about Harriett Tubman, a strong colored woman who didn't "take no stuff," as she used to say.

"Hillie, gal, ah knows there's some sorta movement goin' on, an' ah can't get involved. We can't do it; so Hillie, ya gotta get out there fo' me and yo' momma. We got other chillens to raise and mens to keep. Oberlin College is a great place to start. They was a part o' the Unnergroun' Railroad, you know. Hillie, yo' got ta be strong – but keep those curls tied up, and watch out."

The Pan-American Exposition of 1901 was going to be held in Buffalo, New York, a city near Niagara Falls. My excitement grew into a passion, the closer it got to my May graduation that same year. Aunt Melinda surprised me on graduation day with $200.00, a train ticket to Buffalo, and an introductory letter to Mrs. Mary B. Talbert. How about that!

I arrived in Buffalo after a long train ride, early August, at the Central Terminal Train Station. What a breathtaking end to my journey! The station was exquisite, with glistening floors, a huge clock in the center of this welcoming hall, and the burnished bronze buffalo standing tall, watching over us all. I was exhausted now, only wanting to jump into one of Mrs. Talbert's beds, which Aunt Melinda had reported to be fluffy.

Before I could grab the doorknocker at her Michigan Street home, I heard a choir singing in the red brick church next door. Candles flickered through the multicolored windows. It seemed just the right welcome, as I heard a spirited choir singing. A small dark-skinned young lady peeked through the cracked door of the house, and then opened it wide as the smile on her face.

"Welcome, Missus, to the home of Mr. and Mrs. Talbert."

During the next few weeks, their home was full of people coming and going; having heated discussions about the plight of colored people. The highlight of these conversations was, of course, "the Expo," as they called it. As I listened, the excitement of this historical moment filled my very being.

Someone said, "The President of the United States will be there. Now is the time to demonstrate and let President McKinley know exactly what is happening to colored people in this here country." Many of the twenty or so men continued to shout similar words. Mr. Talbert stood up, waved his massive hand over the room; quieting the most enthusiastic. In a deep, strong voice, Mr. Talbert spoke.

"Now, gentlemen, hold on to your tempers. That is all they need – for us to become boisterous and violent. I realize we have to do something to show our abhorrence of this country's treatment of colored people, and to support the Paris Negro Exhibit that shows the advancement of Negroes since slavery. Mrs. Talbert and I have discussed an idea that might work, at least for a while. My wife's club of about twenty women has volunteered to march in front of the West Amherst gate entrance to the Expo."

"All right, then, all right! Amen!" was repeated several times.

Mrs. Talbert asked me to join her club members a few days later. In late August and early September 1901, we strutted proudly for several hours a day, four days each week. We walked up and down Delaware Avenue, then to the other side of the Expo on Amherst Street.

Mrs. Talbert suggested we take some time off, but warned us to be very careful.

"Enjoy this American wonder," she said to me. "Get lots of information for your first news article." She smiled and so did I.

I was amazed and in awe of this city, seeing the lights in the evening, illuminating the Electric Tower and other buildings as I strolled along the Midway and the Mall. The next afternoon, I was compelled to visit the Manufacturers and Liberal Arts Building to see the Negro Exhibit. My body trembled when I saw all the wonderful things my people had accomplished, from literature and scientific manuals, to inventions, and so much more.

I saw his face first. It was rustic, foreign, with scruffy hair. I thought he was a drunken homeless man. People had warned me about them, too. But he was a small, muscular man, who seemed not to have missed too many meals. His voice came from somewhere else, because it was angry and harsh.

"That President McKinley is no good. Why should he have so much and I nothing? He must die!" Then he turned and looked at me with a fierce scowl. He was so frightful, I ran to the first police officer I could find.

"Mr. Policeman, sir?" I called, trying to keep my composure. "There's a man running around here shouting that he's going to kill the President!"

Ernest Knight was a Buffalo Police Lieutenant; one of the

youngest and brightest, he later told me. Well, he did look good in that uniform, with his dark hair, strong, chiseled jaw and shocking blue eyes. I was surprised at my sudden attraction to him. This was certainly a big no-no.

"No white boys allowed," my momma – and especially Aunt Melinda – used to say all the time. Still, there was something about him. It must have been his kindness and those beautiful teeth.

Ernest saw Hilda approaching. Coming closer, he saw big, brown eyes, a corseted, small waist that bloomed out into a burgundy skirt and fitted jacket. Her blouse was ruffled, just as she was herself.

"Can't get too excited; might lose everything," Ernest thought to himself.

Those black curls came falling to her shoulders from under her square black hat. After swallowing several times, trying to keep his policeman posture, he asked her a few questions about the man. Hilda described him to the last detail. Ernest saw the passion he so desired in a woman – a woman independent and strong-spirited.

"Miss Watt, let's walk towards the Temple of Music. It's quiet there."

"Of course," I replied. I wanted to know more about this man.

We walked and talked; he listened and so did I. He even confided in me that he was mixed, with Irish from his mother and Indian-African from his father. I knew there was something different about him.

I could feel Ernest's uneasiness. He seemed to be on guard during most of our conversation. The crowd became denser.

"So sorry, but I'll have to leave now. I'll meet you an hour at the Delaware entrance. Go there now!" as he kissed my cheek.

People were rushing to meet the President in the greeting line.

"Maybe its time now, Mr. President!" the voice said. The nerves all over my body quivered when I heard that angry voice cry out loud.

"Ernest! Ernest!" I screamed with all my strength. He turned and saw the man from my detailed description. The man was quiet and subdued now.

"I hope he is not the one," I cried softly.

The gun was black and huge, like the sound it made vibrating throughout the Temple of Music, just after he looked into my eyes. Ernest ran panting towards him, grabbing his wrist, but not before the two bullets found their massive target. He and a man named James Parker (we learned later) wrestled the shooter to the floor, as the third shot missed.

The Temple of Music was a hollow place now. The lights that once lit up the world were now dimming, and then gone. President William McKinley, the twenty-fifth President of the United States, died fourteen days after surgery. This was done in an operating room that had no electricity, by a gynecologist and an obstetrician, one hour and twenty minutes after he was shot.

It was late October, a cool, gorgeous afternoon in Mrs. Talbert's parlor. The Talberts had kindly rented me a room in their home. They even influenced Mr. Calloway to let me work at his new newspaper office, called *The Gazette and Guide.*

Many thoughts ran through my mind that day as I finished editing a story that would soon be published. I tried not to think of Ernest, but… I still felt his warmth and remembered his face.

Vinnie, the housekeeper, answered the soft knock on the door. She led him into the parlor. His strong hand stroked my hair as

I turned, startled, looking into his blue eyes.

"I told them who I really am and still kept my job. Now I want to know more about you," he said, as Vinnie closed the parlor doors.

This story was for a contest in the Buffalo News. They gave us an outline to follow. We had to write about the Pan-American Exposition in Buffalo, on the day President McKinley was assassinated. We had to use the names of the characters given, and write why and how these two were in the same place at the same time. We could use historical places and people, but could use our imaginations and change some things. The church is still there. A garden and a plaque are where Mrs. Talbert's home used to be.

It was an exciting challenge to write this story. I didn't win, but I tried. Hope you will enjoy it.

Love... Priscilla

January 23, 2007

STEP IV   FAMILY: MIX TENDERLY

With warm memories of loved ones; honoring the lives
of the living; remembering good old days gone by;
some passion and a bit of humor, we embrace and mix
affectionately the lives of family, friends and community.

Psalm 25:6
***"Remember O Lord, thy tender mercies and thy
loving kindness; for they have been ever of old"***

ALABAMA RED CLAY

Attalla/Gadsden… red ruddy hills
Of Alabama is where I'm from.
One side white from slavery,
One side dark from Africa.
A slice of Native-American,
Makes me milky, milk chocolate in between
Is where I'm from.

Born in Grandma's bed, (where did Grandpa sleep?)
Covered with great quilts that told secret stories,
The bed that bore babies and hid deaths,
That gave us comfort from the storms,
That held us tight from the fear
Is where I'm from.

Scrubbed in Grandma's tin tub,
In front of the warm stove;
The tub that washed white folks' clothes,
Made corn liquor and other things
Is where I'm from.

Like blackberry pie, all hot and
Juicy, sweet and oozing together,
For others to devour…
Piece…by…piece.

A PRIMEVAL PLACE

Around the corner, on this dusty road,
Lush Alabama mountains rise up
Leading us to our family gathering,
Where we celebrate once more someone's life.
A life filled with children, sunshine, summer storms,
Fig trees, pecans, bare feet, births, deaths, and other things.
There were stories in this life
That made us giggle, laugh out loud,
Cry and wonder sometimes,
About the "colored" signs everywhere.
We were forever sitting on that screened porch, those
Hot, sticky summers, listening to the squeaking door,
Waiting for something to happen.
　　　　　　The thunderstorms came quickly each day
　　　　　　And passed just as suddenly, leaving
　　　　　　Steamy streets that dried up
　　　　　　Like a ten-minute coffee break.
　　　　　There were hidden spaces on the back
　　　　　　Screened porch, that hid corn whiskey,
　　　　　　Jams, tomatoes, peaches in jars, snuff in cans,
　　　　　　Pots, secrets, and wonderful old things.
I used to look at the pecan trees, thinking
How deliciously comforting they were,
But reminding me of the hanging man in Jet
And the "Strange Fruit" of Billie Holiday.
Aunt Lou's smooth mahogany skin was like
Her furniture, stationed all over this warm house,
Smelling like fried chicken and cobbler pie,
 Homemade cakes, mixed by hand, licked by us.
　　　　　　We buried her in the Green plot, in Alabama,
　　　　　　In the still-colored, now private, cemetery,
　　　　　　Next to my grandparents, my Uncles and Aunt "T"
　　　　　　Whose grave was not completely filled in, as if
　　　　　　The rain had moved the dirt around.
I looked at each one's marker, feeling the rich African blood
Flowing through my veins,

Thinking they had seen me, touched me, kissed me
And held me in their arms.
Fear suddenly seizes me, tears fall on my face
Because I am nearer to the top
Of the generational ladder now.
They think I'm crying for her,
But I'm really crying for myself.

MAMA'S WORLD

Her world was a city that
Smelled like hard work, slaughtered animals,
Scotch and smoke.
Her world was Willert Park,
Four rooms, one bath on Jefferson
Avenue, with the only tree on the block.

Her world was card playing,
Numbers, 641, 452; ten-cent straight, nickel in the box…
House parties, card parties,
Johnny Walker Red and fried Dixie Peach.
Her world was life at a third,
No banks, no checks; cash only…for hot clothes, hot food,
And always hot fun.

My Mama celebrated everything:
Birthdays, graduations, weddings, births, deaths, and
Just because it was a good day,
Taking pictures to prove it.
She went to Polly's on Jefferson Avenue, Kerns on William Street,
Of course, Memory Lane on Howard.

Her Sundays were like Thanksgivings every week.
When the holidays came,
We decorated and celebrated with homemade wine,
Home brew, neighbors and friends.

In her earlier life, she sat
On a stool every day,
Cigarette hanging on the side of her mouth,
Curling hair at $2.50 a head.
That took good care of the
Two children she loved.

Then the Lord blessed her with a husband

We called Mac, who wanted respect, a comfortable home,
Good food and love.
Mama gave it to him.
And Mac gave her what she needed too – a loving home and peace.

Mother always gave us lessons of life:
"Don't put your hands on your hips when you talk to me," or
"Always wear clean underwear," and
"When you send someone a card, please put a dollar in it."

So I celebrate my mother's life,
Because she brought so much joy into my world,
And the hearts of others who knew her.

For Mama... Eloise Green McPherson

HAPPY DADDY RICHARD DAY

The train at Central Terminal came panting
Into the station,
Steam covering the massive wheels,
As it roared to a halt and hiss.

I was so nervous as I squeezed
My mother's hand,
Not really wanting to go… but we did.
We were the only kids going away
This summer – on a real train.

Settling down in the padded seats,
Looking at the black men dressed
In their fine suits and caps,
Making us feel so important,
As we opened the shoe box

                Of fried chicken, cookies and other stuff,

Trying not to drop crumbs on our new clothes.
My heart thumped rapidly through my dress,
Knowing that I would soon see this man
Whose voice I remembered, from the phone.

You were stern, polite and happy to see us.
You asked us Daddy Richard things,
About school, our friends, and report cards.
You made plans for our days,
And tucked us in at night.
You gave us vitamins and orange juice
For breakfast.
Aunt Flossie changed our clothes, fed us,
And sent us out to play in the afternoon.
It was a little hard getting used to, at first;
But at least we knew what Daddies
Were supposed to do.

We were proud as we returned
To the unrestricted home in Willert Park;
Telling our friends about the healthy meals,
Our trips on a plane and Amusement Park,
And about being in the house
Before the lights came on.

I called you many names throughout my life:
Father, Daddy Richard, Daddy, Dad…
I called you in my daydreams,
And especially in my nightmares.
You've always been there for me,
Helping me, guiding me spiritually,
And strengthening me even when
You said "No."

And whenever I hear a train whistle,
I feel the steam of the engine and
See the silhouette of the man
From the phone, who loves me.

DEAR DADDY RICHARD

Saturday, September 10, 2009

Dear Daddy Richard,

When I was a little girl, to me, you were bigger and larger than life. You were grand. Your voice so deep and your hands so strong, I guess from playing all that golf and tennis. Always tennis rackets and golf balls all over the house. And those cigars! You loved those cigars; I always thought that you had to smoke cigars to be a grandfather.

I'll remember those fun and scary summer nights of storytelling and of catching fireflies in jars, and the good smells coming from Aunt Flossie's kitchen in the mornings. I'll remember our long, long talks on the phone, how wonderful and enlightening for me. You were my grandfather and friend, and I'll miss you so much. I love you. I've asked God to keep you and to watch over you and to bless you always.

Chari, granddaughter.

****

When I remember my Dad, I remember he was a good father. I remember going to his house as a young boy and smelling the sweet aroma of his pipe. I tried my best to emulate him. I watched his mannerisms. I tried on his hats. I walked in his shoes.

I remember the bedtime stories he told me, that were meant to scare me; but at the end, I would always ask him to tell me another.

He was a good father, and taught me lessons about life, and was always encouraging. Now my earthly father is with my heavenly father... and now more than ever, I remember the words he loved so much. "God grant me the serenity..."

Mark A. Green, your son

****

For my Daddy,

We called you Daddy Richard for a long time. You gave us our first vitamins and
wholesome breakfasts, when we visited for the summer. You took us on our first airplane
ride over Cleveland, and my children, too, on a trip to Alabama. You bought me my first
pair of stockings and gloves for church. You showed me how to shave under my arms,
to be a young lady. You taught us not to follow the crowd. Lastly, you taught us God's
love, by the ways you taught and loved us.

The last time I saw you, I was going home after a few weeks. You said "I am blessed!" as you threw up your arms. "I don't know what I would do without you and Mark. I love you. Goodbye."
Now I say, "So long," because I know I will see you one day in your Heavenly Home.

I celebrate your life – I LOVE YOU!

Your daughter, Priscilla Green Hill

"T"

Her hair was white as second-day snow,
Scarce, like winter trees, after a storm,
And soft as cotton candy in summer.

Her smile was warm and comforting;
Like those cookies she use to make,
Pinwheels, oatmeal and sugar,
All wrapped in waxed paper, with love,
That secured us on the train back home.

Those summers in Cleveland she would
Interrupt our play to wash us, feed us, hug us,
And return us to those hot, summer days.

"T" always had her daily chores;
From ironing sheets, shirts and shorts,
To cooking meals that included
Delicious, decadent desserts.
The warmth of her being
Was not only arrayed on her person,
But savoured in the preparation of her food.

I now see her softly-lined face glowing
With deep, inquisitive eyes, filled with her spirit,
A spirit that shows me what real strength
In a woman truly means.

I wonder has she been fulfilled?
I wonder if she knows how much
She has meant to all of us?

GINA: THE GIFT

Dancing the Rubber Leg must have set it off,
Or the luscious feast Mom cooked that day.
The sharp pain hit hard just as I sucked
On that fried-chicken bone.

There was a succession of thrusting the pains away,
 And heaving mounds of macaroni and cheese, greens down my
throat.
It was my last supper as my mom's little girl.

The miracle I carried in me was craving
To be released into the world.
I knew you were a precious gift,
So I named you Regina – Queen –
The European version.
My young mind had not opened up
To my African heritage yet.
I wanted your name to sound
Strong and proud, like you have become.

My Queen tore out of me
Like it was Friday night at the Apollo.
A big, blue-brown, wide-eyed wonder,
Ready for the world,
Born a gift, my immortality
And my link to your father.

As you grew, I looked into your eyes
And saw something far beyond your years.
You were my "Earth Angel," my "Cherry Pie,"
My "Still in the Night."

You have become the woman I admire,
The mother I cherish and the friend I need.
I remember the aura of you, as you stepped into a room
And I, slouching, began to rise up,

Remembering, you taught me that I could too.

You are now a woman of the world,
Who lets nothing stand in your way.
But I especially remember that
Throughout these forty years,
The greatest gift you have given me
Is your tender, requited love.

CHARI: MY WILDFLOWER

The seed of love that brought you to me
Was something I thought would never be.
The tears I cried, the pain inside...

But there is a time for everything,
And you were destined to be mine,
That October morning.
Those bright eyes, opened to the world
Looking like a Cochise,
All curly-headed, caramel-coloured,
With lollipop lips that whispered sweet sounds,
And tiny feet that turned sideways.

You've become the light that flickers
But never burns out.
You have an aura that shows
How proud you are.
Your beauty hides deep inside,
Escaping through your words,
Through your faith,
Through your eyes.

You give me strength from conflict,
And compassion from forgiveness.
You are my wildflower, growing wild
But free; full of life's hues,
Embracing the world.

Thanks for giving me your unending love
And passion for living.

My Family

Gibran   My beautiful baby boy, bringing us so much joy twenty-five years ago, squatting in front of the lens, taking the first pictures of your life. You have special talents that have yet to be discovered. Life took you places you never thought of, as you and Mildred gave to us our first great-grandson, Kahlile . You make us so proud of who you have become.

Ashley   You are the granddaughter who sniffed your turned up nose, fell asleep in Nanette's doorway, and loved fast cars; whose stubbornness brought many time-outs. You are now a beautiful, young woman with special talents, whose voice still tickles my ears and makes me laugh. You are a grandma friend who I can chill out with but who can teach me wonderful lessons of life.

Julian   My grandson, God's surprise gift to us, now a teen of ages, clicking on the "CP's," computers, X Boxes, cell phone and reading books about the art of war; always trying to find out the workings of the world. I used to get a letter once in a while, but now we communicate through texting.

Kahlile   Our brand new son great as you are, your Angel breathed into you the breath of life, as you gazed into your mother's face, as you saw yourself in your father's eyes, coming into this world, into a family from different places, filling up our wonderful spaces of life. "Can you say "Lala" yet?"

My Family Growing Anew

Wiley, my husband, who gave you all to me six years ago.

Trey   Meeting you my new grandson, for the first time, you were so cool and still is; with a family that shines like a bright flame, preparing you for manhood and survival in this challenging world. You even send us cards on Grandparents Day!

Cathy   You are a mother, my daughter now, who stands tall and strong, who loves the joys of living, who gives love and support to your son, but lets him know his limitations, who sends us messages of inspiration to uplift our days.

Adriane You are an aunt, my daughter now, who holds Trey dear to her heart, who shares the love of a mother, who makes the best of life for older friends and family, who seeks the beauty in old buildings created long ago.

"If I could give you all that you desire, I would, but instead I give you love." Lala

A LETTER FROM IAN

5/11/08

Dear Aunt Cilla,

> *Hey, how's it going in New York? It's okay here in Cleveland. This is Ian, writing you your May letter.*

> *Hi, what's new in Buffalo? Nothing new here, but I went to a band field trip. My school band went to a school on the west side and performed and received awards. As you know, I play the keyboard, and I performed a song called "Happy Feet". I received a "Superior" award. I was so happy that day! I'm going to be performing at our school spring concert. My first concert was a little scary, but as you get used to it, it's okay.*

> *My brother Larry just had his first birthday. His birthday was on April 10th. We had a home party and it was a blast. I took pics of the party and had fun. He has got badder since then. He does sneaky things. At his party we did different things like: face painting, pin the tail on the donkey, horseshoes, piñata, and much more. It was fun and we really enjoyed it.*

> *HAPPY MOTHER'S DAY! How was your Mother's Day? Mine was great. I woke up this morning and cooked my mom some breakfast. I gave her a crystal with a flower in the middle that says "Love". Then I went to church. And I'm with you as you're reading this, this moment. What happens now...?*

> *Well, that's all I have for now. I can't wait to see you, and hope that your Mother's Day stays blessed, and I love YOU and UNCLE WILEY, and I'm praying for you.*

P.S. I hope Sharie gets better,

> *Love,*
> *Ian*

AUTUMN LOVE

We were truly blessed,
Meeting in the autumn of our lives.
A time of year that is beautiful,
Cool, and free.
A time to warm our hearts,
And prepare for winter's chill.

We fell in love on a spring night,
Bringing to us the closeness and
Bewilderment of new love.

He came crashing into my heart,
As he crashed into my house.
All I could say was
"I hope you like music."

Sitting coolly on concrete steps in yellow shorts,
I waited to be introduced to my new neighbor,
Who had a nice smile, friendly handshake,
And a little nervousness about him.

Then I turned my legs sideways
So he could get a better view.
A breeze caressed the hair on my neck,
Making me wonder… hmmm…
Naw! But I knew he liked music.

Two years it took
On the journey to that cool night,
On the harbor, overlooking the river,
Where I ached for his touch,
For the warmth of his body.

Ooooh that night!
He was so fine
Like a diamond mine

As delicious as expensive wine
And I wanted him to be mine... mine... mine!

As he finally took my hand,
Leading me to a place I've never been.
So I stayed... and I stayed... I stayed.

He was the one all the while.
I looked in all the spaces of my abode,
In all the detour,
In all the pain,
In all the regrets,
In all the memories,
Then I found him...
Right at my house,
            On my mind,
                        In my heart.
I knew it, though...
I knew he was the one,
Who'd hold me close,
Whisper, "I love you" in the curve
Of my neck,
Bringing me the passion
I've sought a lifetime,
Making me... finally... complete

*To my wonderful Husband who has made
my life full of love and joy. I thank God
for you...*

Your loving Wife, Priscilla Hill

GLADYS AND CARRIE: THE BIRDCAGE

"Aunt Gladys," sighed Jackie, one of Gladys' many "children, "that's a real nice birdcage! But I didn't know you had a bird."

"Hee hee," snickered Gladys.

Aunt Gladys and her husband John had no biological children in this Pershing Street neighborhood, but all the children belonged to them. She was a short, plump, dark-skinned woman, whose age was unknown; but she seemed to stay ageless for as long as we knew her. That one tooth on the side of her mouth could devour any food she wanted to eat, from fried chicken to pigs' feet. And it didn't interfere with the smile that warmed our hearts. John was tall, weathered brown; he didn't let Gladys work, except to keep a pleasant, clean house, full of love and good food. That's what she gave him.

One of her favorite things to do (besides cooking) was to bargain shop at flea markets, estate sales, street sales or any other kind of sale. Her partner in sales was Carrie, Gladys' best and oldest friend. Carrie was dark-brown-skinned, a large woman with big tender hands and feet and a sparkle in her eyes. Carrie had four children when I first met her. When the grandchildren came along, they called her Nana.

Gladys and Carrie had many things in common, like shopping; but the first thing you saw was their humor. Boy, did they love to laugh hysterically, and loved it best when you laughed with them! Sometimes when we just stopped by their porches for a visit, they would be cackling and giggling about something or other.

On this summer morning ("Early is better"), Gladys and Carrie decided to go to the Flea Market on Broadway. Gladys couldn't drive, but Carrie could wheel that hoopty anywhere they wanted to go, at any time. They searched and searched; got tired and had a snack; and searched some more.

On the last look around – you see, they didn't want to buy stuff they didn't really need – Gladys spotted something that "circled and curved this way and that," was how she put it.

"Hey, Carrie, look at that thing. Ain't that gorgeous?"

"What is it?" Carrie asked quizzically. "Looks to me like a cage of some sort. Well, it's kinda big, don't ya say? It's pretty though, kinda like a antique."

"Hey, how much?" hollered Gladys at the scrubby old man whose skin was so red, it was peeling on his nose and cheeks.

"Gimme ten dollars," answered the man, wiping his forehead with a dirty handkerchief.

"Whatcha think we are, rich or something?" said Carrie.

"Okay, nine dollars."

"Naw, come on, man," Gladys smiled, showing that one tooth, barely hanging on.

It was getting late. The sun was glowing red and their shadows were longer now.

Impatient and thinking he would lose this sale altogether, the man said, "Oh, shoot. Okay, you know what? Take it for five dollars." He was pleased with that move. Now he could get a real nice dinner.

"Three!" shouted Carrie back, knowing this was the last offer.

"Gotcha!" The man smiled as he said this, knowing he had found this old relic on somebody's garbage day, though now he'd have a good lunch.

The prize of the day was home at last. The children gathered around to see just what it was.

"Aunt Gladys, what is it?" asked Toni.

"Girl, ain't that the most beautiful birdcage you ever wanna see?"

"But Aunt Gladys… Nana, you don't even have a bird," Jeannie said, with a frown.

Chari, Gina, Betty, Phoebe, Val, Toni, and some of the other children who gathered around to see this "new thing", started rolling with laughter, coughing, eyes tearing, pointing to Gladys and Carrie's prize birdcage.

"Well, what's so funny?" said Carrie, a little irritated. "You all crazy! This here is a birdcage. We ain't got no bird, but me and Gladys will be on our way early in the morning to find a bird… or two. NOW!" She rolled her eyes, but sneaked a smile in there too.

Aunt Gladys looked at Carrie, closed her eyes, sucked on that one tooth and said, "What time, Carrie?"

The kids snickered quietly, whispering about what kind of bird would they get? one or two? what color? which ones can be caged, and who gonna clean up their mess? as they walked home for evening supper.

HOMEGOING AND HOMECOMINGS

Last week was a time of funerals for me (Homegoings, as we called them). My childhood friend Aviva and my Aunt Linda passed during this week. We honored their lives and grieved their deaths. Both were beautiful ceremonials about people who touched my life.

On Wednesday, I saw old friends in Buffalo, as we celebrated the life of a friend to many, mother and sister. She had also been a supporter of the Sickle Cell Charity, a member of the Mary B. Talbert Club and their associates; the Federated Colored Women's Clubs; and a devoted member of her church. I saw people who had just returned to the Buffalo area, and so many more whom I hadn't seen in years. We exchanged numbers and promised to keep in touch, which we never do.

In Alabama, the next day, my family celebrated the Homegoing of another person who had an impact on my life. She was also a mother, friend, and the last matriarch of my family. During my visit I met, once again, after fifteen years, cousins, nieces, nephews, who had grown up with their own families, some with new partners. And with great surprise and honor, I met the oldest of all the family. What a Homecoming this was!

He was a fascinating, intelligent, agile, handsome man of 86 years. We had always heard of the time when he flew his own plane over my grandmother's burial site in 1986. As we talked over the pound cake his wife had sent with him and his son, from Jacksonville, Florida, he retold parts of his life story. Our young cousin, Kiki, who is addicted to the Internet, showed us information of his registration into the Air Force.

Cousin Tom, as we called him, relayed his involvement with the Tuskegee Airmen. He had been accepted into the Air Force with a secret security clearance, even though he didn't even have a birth certificate. He said that when he was born, his parents didn't have the money to pay the doctor, and so his birth was not documented. Later he tried to obtain one and was refused. But because of his intelligence about the mechanics of the airplane and communications, he was accepted.

Cousin Thomas taught the pilots how to use the communication in their planes; he maintained the planes and had many other jobs. He was given security clearance when the Tuskegee Airmen flew missions over Russia and Japan during WWII. He directed them while they were in flight.

Cousin Thomas was a soldier who stayed in the background, but because of his knowledge, their missions were successful. We have always heard these stories and felt very proud, not knowing how utterly important his life has been. Cousin Thomas has always been so humble, saying he did what he had to do. What a Homegoing for my aunt, my childhood friend, and Homecoming for an honored cousin!

Maybe this time we'll keep in touch.

MY DARLING DAUGHTER, STEPHANIE

God is good and full of Grace.
He knew when it was time
To take you Home,
Leaving my heart heavy,
But filled with memories of you.
I used to put your picture on
The refrigerator and hold you close
In my wallet, telling everyone
How cute you were.
I loved making you homemade goodies
And hurt when you were in pain.
I worried about your health,
And held your head close to my heart
When you needed me most.
All that has ended,
Because you are in a better place now;
But Mama will always miss you.

… Loreda …

FOR LENORE BETHEL COOPER, IN REMEMBRANCE

I thank you, Lenore, for not encouraging me
To pursue a career in painting.
I thank you, though, for your gentle strength,
Your patient guidance,
For your love of the Arts,
As you guided me to create
A new life.

You helped me publish a Chapbook of poems,
Created an altar for my mother,
And one for me.
Displayed my art and poetry
On the walls of Locust Street
For everyone to see.
When I went looking for myself,
You helped me find her in the arts.
 Giving me "aha!" moments,
Gently nudging me, saying, "Try this."

You leave a space in our hearts
That can never be filled.
A legacy that created life
In people, on walls, and churches.
Giving us precious moments,
When we etched our names
On those tiles of life, forever lasting.

Miss you.
Priscilla and Wiley, June 8, 2009

THE SIZZLING SUMMER OF NAOMI AND THE ICEMAN

We used to hear the rough, whiskey-voiced, middle-aged man calling:

"Iceman. iceman, comin' roun', if you need some ice, come on down. Who wants ice-cold ice from this iceman? Yo, Miss Emma Jean, I'm coming! I know you need some ice today!"

Miss Emma Jean lived across the street from us, in a small blue wooden house, with her six kids. We all scrambled around him begging for chips of ice, though most of us lived in Willert Park Courts and had the newest refrigerators, which we called "fridge".

"Stand back, you little dusty, nappy-headed kids!"

The creaky, weathered wheels under his battered old truck, turned slowly up Jefferson Avenue. There were huge blocks of ice piled high on scruffy haystacks. We grabbed for the ice chips he finally gave us.

"Now, git on, chillen. Hey, Johnny, and you, Spanky, watch my truck an' don't eat no mo' ice, ya hea'?"

The strong Iceman threw a two-claw hook on a block of ice, about the size of four-year-old Lil Junior, and hefted it up on his massive shoulder. His bowlegs and slew feet clumped on up the steps to Miss Emma Jean's porch, then disappeared into the house.

Three times a week, the Iceman came up Jefferson Avenue and the surrounding streets of this Buffalo east-side neighborhood, on those hot days that never seemed to end. All those years we never even knew his name, until...

The Iceman, born Nathaniel Owens, Jr., was a sixty-year-old

father of two. His sun-baked, rugged skin, short muscular build, and calloused hands proved that he had worked hard and long, ever since he and Mattie drove from Attalla, Alabama, thirty-five years earlier, looking for a better life.

Though he couldn't find the work he wanted, Mr. Albert Cottrell, a lawyer, hired him to do odd jobs. They soon became good friends; the time they spent together, even for a few minutes, became a solace for them both. It was Mr. Cottrell who encouraged Nathaniel to take over the ice business.

One hot day in May, in 1949, Mr. Owens saw a new family move their meager belongings into a rundown gray house, on Monroe Street.

"Good blessings to you all. Need some ice this morning, suh?"

"No!" answered the light-brown-skinned, burly father, scrunching up his face.

"Okay, maybe tomorrow."

The next day was in the upper eighties and humid.

"I know they need some ice today," said the Iceman, as he knocked on the front door. When the door finally opened, he saw a tall, beautiful, cinnamon-colored young lady in her teens… with bruises on her neck and arms, that hung from a flowered summer dress.

"I thought y'all might need some ice today, ma'am. I'm the Iceman, as they call me, but my name is Mr. Nathaniel Owens, Jr."

"I'm Naomi, and these are my two sisters. They're shy. But we don't have any money today."

"Oh, Miss Naomi, I've got extra ice every day. Y'all can

have it, or I gotta throw it away."

"Oh, yes. Yes, we'll take it," in her soft voice.

The Iceman brought the large chunk of ice and placed it in the battered old icebox. "Thank you so much. We'll give you something when we can. Here, take these cookies I just baked."

Naomi closed the door slowly, feeling the warmth of the Iceman. "Just like Grandpa Gene."

The heat had cooled down a bit on that Thursday afternoon when the Iceman met Naomi and her sisters at the door.

"My lawyer friend, Mr. Cottrell, need some help in his office. Wanna job?"

Naomi was hesitant, but excited. "Mr. Owens, if I could have time to send the kids off to school in the morning, I'll take it."

"Great!" said the Iceman emphatically.

Naomi worked diligently the rest of the summer, filing papers, learning many skills and making a few friends. She had to hide some of her wages from her drunken father to buy goodies for the kids.

The Iceman didn't come, on this particular September morning. Everyone thought he was finished for the rest of the year.

The summer was finally over, too. We were back in school #31. The weather had cooled down considerably on that late September Saturday, when we sneaked over to the Plaza Show. Walking home, we saw the Jones Funeral Home; and all someone had to say was, "Let's see somebody dead!"

There they were, all lined up in every room, looking pasty and real dead. In the third room, the body was covered in a blue veil over the casket. Aviva read the inscription. His name was Nathaniel Owens, Sr., husband of Mae, father of Nathaniel Jr., PhD, Phyllis and Francis, grandfather of six.

We slowly eased closer.

"Wow!" we screamed all together. "It's the Iceman!"

Then we ran down the concrete steps, onto Jefferson Avenue, to our Willert Park Court, to tell the other kids the news.

At work the next Monday, Mr. Cottrell took Naomi aside and told her softly, with tears in his eyes, "Naomi, Mr. Owens passed away in his sleep Thursday morning." The ache in her heart was great and she wept.

Several weeks later, Mr. Cottrell said to Naomi, "Mr. Owens had a substantial estate, and he left you $20,000 to help you complete your college education."

Four years after that, Naomi walked proudly across the University stage, as her sisters watched and cried. Even her sobered dad was there. But she knew the Iceman was also looking down, and was very pleased.

MY SISTER... MY FRIEND... NANETTE

We are so connected!
The same Lola who loves
And blesses you, blesses me too!
The same man we call V
Loves both of us, you see?
Wow! We are so connected!

We are so connected...
The same sun that shines on you
Shines on me.
Even the wind encircles the trees,
Whispering to the leaves,
Swirling around corners, under porches,
To get from you to me.

We are so connected...
Imagine two snowflakes
Drifting silently downward,
Softly around us...
One kisses my cheek,
The other caresses your hair.

We are so connected...
Remember the silent thoughts,
In the still of the night,
That permeated our minds,
Ones that cried out to be heard
And you called me...

We are so connected...
Remember daydreaming on the porch
On those hot, summer August nights?
Of coulda-beens or how-comes,
Turning them into nightmares
And a busy signal
'Cause we were calling out to each other
Wow! We are so connected!

LOLA

I have been truly blessed having sister/friends. You came into my life where I didn't think I would ever let a woman friend enter. Our lives were in the middle of changes, like our ages, but you always had that spiritual aura about you. When we went to New Covenant to worship, we cried and cried, like we were truly sinners.

Somehow the Lord put his loving arms around us and held us tight, because we got through it alive and kicking; but not as high, now.

You always seemed to know when I needed you, and would pray for me and with me, especially when I didn't know how.

The Lord put you here for a blessed purpose. You have affected many lives, like mine; teaching me how to pray, directing my path.

Your son, Ronald, who recently passed, and Corey's father, were blessed to have you by their sides.

You linked Nanette and me together, forever. The Lord knew what he was doing when he created you.

Even now, through your pain and trials, you still have the faith of Job, the stamina of Esther, and the belief of Ruth. I could go on, but you are humble.

"Trust in the Lord with all thy heart
And lean not on thine own understanding;
In all thy ways acknowledge him,
And he shall direct thy paths." Proverbs 3:5,6

Bless you, my sister/friend,

Priscilla

A PORCH STORY, FOR AVIVA
1944-1955
For Aviva's 60th Birthday

Our first "porch" was a step at the front door, downstairs, in the Willert Park Courts. You see, everybody's got a porch somewhere.

Well, it didn't look like any other porches you see on peoples' houses. There were eight porch steps in our little "cul-de-sac," or "courtyard," as we called it. Each one had a wrought-iron rail on one side and a concrete overhang. We sat on the doorstep, on the rail, and on the bottom step.

We moved around from porch-step to porch-step, depending on who was home, who had goodies, who had food or new toys, or who was the most popular at that particular time. Our moms planted flowers, cabbage, greens, tomatoes, and other vegetables in our communal garden.

The hallways smelled scrumptious on Sundays and holidays, since everybody kept their doors open most of the time. Before the holidays, some of our moms and the dads (those still there), and "uncles" made homebrewed beer and deliciously decadent wine (which we just had to sip), to be ready for Thanksgiving and Christmas.

Each summer, the kids would choose a porch-step and a game to play. It seems like "playing school" was the first I remember. We lined up the kids on the hallway steps, according to their grades. Next came "house"; we used to make pies out of mud, used weeds to make peas and greens. Sometimes we actually ate our play food and made our mothers mad as hell.

As we grew older each summer, the games became marbles, jacks and ball, jump rope, hand-jive. Then came knife and card games. We played tonke, where the loser would get an Indian burn (twisting an arm in different directions), or knuckles, where you got your knuckles hit with the cards. Wow! That hurt!

I do remember when the card games stopped; we began to go our separate ways. People moved away into houses, (the Jacksons were first); kids grew up, got jobs, went into the service, married or had kids of their own.

Our porch-step changed so quickly and was over too soon. Then it was time to change places or move on.

Our porch-step stories of fifty years ago seem like only yesterday. If only for a brief moment, we dreamed, had hopes, goals of mountains to conquer, places to see and things to experience. Some of us did! Like you, Aviva!

I thank you for being a part of my porches.

Love,
Cilla

A GATHER OF GIRLFRIENDS

Lord, you know when I'll be coming,
And I have some questions… if you don't mind.
Lord, can I be an Angel
And help people with their plans?
Can I sit upon a cirrus cloud
And gaze down on the table
Where my girlfriends gather?
I know their faces will be long,
Because they love me, you see.
I made them laugh and think about
Wonderful things, didn't I, Lord?

Can I tickle Erlene, since her laughter,
Deep from her belly, will get them started?
Then I'll tickle each long face till
I won't have to tickle anymore.

Lord, can I taste a piece of Carolyn's
Pound cake, sitting on her patio?
Can I get DuRutha (my got-your-back girl)
To scare the daylights out of Barbara,
That dark-eyed Haitian girl, and make her laugh out loud?

Lord, can I stick my fingers in Sonia's
Dimples, before she goes to a restaurant?
Can I take a look at that "orra" girl Denise's
Long, pretty legs, as she walks away from me?

Can I sneak into Vinnette's kitchen,
To see what her "special seasonings" are?
Lord, I know I'm asking a lot,
And I'm not even there yet.

Can I bathe in Althea's big, black
Whirlpool tub, surrounded by
Candlelight, sipping on her clam chowder ?

And Lord, one last thing…
Can I send them a poem once in a while
To remind them of me?

Thanks… Cilla

CRYSTAL'S 50TH BIRTHDAY

Crystal... an Uncrowned Queen,
Breaking the glass ceiling every day
With her style, her presence, her attitude.
But one day, back in her day,
She was thinking of the meaning of her life at thirteen.

She flopped down on her creaky old bed,
Trying to avoid the pop-up springs,
Trying to be a real good girl,
Thinking of the meaning of her life.

Suddenly the BOOK opened
To Ecclesiastes 3:15, and she saw:
"Everything that happens,
Has happened before...
And all that will be,
Has already been."
God does everything
Over and over again.

After several minutes of "introspection,
(You know she was a thinker),
She decided to do nothing. Know why?
'Cause it's been done before!

Ma-a-a-a! I will not get up this morning,
Take a bath or braid my hair... know why?
'Cause its been done before!

Ma-a-a-a! I will not wash dishes, clean the kitchen,
Or iron any more shirts, sheets and pillowcases... know why?
'Cause it's been done before!

Now Ma was real quiet, until
Crystal sucked her teeth and said:
Ma-a-a-a! I will not go to any
More meetings with you again...know why?

'Cause it's been done before!
Wanting to teach Crystal the meaning of life,
Ma said, "Well I guess you won't have
To eat anymore, either... know why?
'Cause that's been done before, too.

And you'd better not suck your teeth
One more time...know why?
'Cause I'm gonna knock them
Right down your throat.

By the way, Crystal, (as she cleaned her switch),
Let me show you something
That's been done before,
And I know will be done
Over and over again!"

BEFORE I KNEW JESUS, I KNEW MICHAEL JACKSON

ABC... it's easy, it's like counting up to three...

And the melody of my life.

Ponytails, long and thick,

Hot summer days,

Watermelon nights,

Cold Spring Buffalo New York 1970

Everything everyday was good, even in this old used-up inner city

...It was all beautiful to me.

From tomboy to boyfriends,

Sunday school to sleepovers and of course, Michael

Jackson and the Jackson 5... my first true love

Singing simple melody...

Bubble-gum smacking, hot-pants wearing, Afros, dashikis, hoola-hoopin' and barbecuin'.

A town where everyone knew everyone else and they all knew your mother.

Suede jackets and rabbit coats, stripes, plaids and white patent leather knee high boots...
we were doin' it!

So proud to be a black girl in my black world

Nothing was better

Willert Park Christmases and how GRAND they were, especially with how little we had.

I may not have known Jesus, but within these honey-sweet memories, He always knew me!

And that's how easy love can be...

- Chari

STEP V   PREPARING FOR THE FEAST:
SOME EXTRA TREATS

Good stuff that I didn't know what to do with except mix them together all by themselves; sprinkling special spices and adding a little color.

Romans: 3:4
"There is no difference, for all have sinned and fall short of the glory of God and are justified freely by His Grace"

BACK IN THE DAY

My world was sweet as a chocolate valentine
As red as Alabama clay.
My world was secure as my grandmother's lap
But stung like her switch on my legs.

My world was a city that smelled of hard work,
Slaughtered animals, Scotch and smoke.
My world was Willert Park, four rooms, one bath
On Jefferson Avenue, with the only tree on the block.
My world was card-playing, numbers, 641-452:
Ten-cent straight, nickel in the box, and...

House parties, Johnny Walker Red, fried Dixie Peach
And fries with vinegar, at the Wil-Pine.
My world was life at a third... no banks, no checks,
Cash only, for hot clothes, hot food and
Always hot fun!

Then my world started changing!
I could hear it! feel it! Like the background music
At the Broadway, Plaza, and Roxie Shows.
My world was "Earth Angel, will you be mine?",
When I found love for the first time.
My world became "Stagger Lee" and the Midnighters,
Who shouted loudly from those long sleek coffin-like
Stereos in our living rooms.

My life went from "cowboys and girls, baby dolls to boys,"
From Matadors to the Pythons,
From Crystal Beach to Lasalle Park.

My world was the "good old days," or so we thought;
'Cause we listened to the Hound Dog howl on WUFO
Giving us Jackie, Ruth, Fats, Etta and Clyde McPhatter,
Sending our music soaring like birds...
Plucked by hawks,

Changing our rhythm and blues, our rock and roll
To blue-eyed soul;
Still, we danced the Skipe, the Chicken,
The Mashed Potato,
And slow-dragged into the night
Until our hair napped up on one side.

*I was born on Valentine's Day in Alabama. The poem is about my
life, mostly as a teenager in the 1950s and 1960s.*

It was the first poem written by me that I shared with the public.

*I was recovering from breast cancer surgery, a mastectomy, and
wanted to share some of my life with my children and grandchildren.*

Priscilla Y. Parker, June 2001

WHO IS <u>THEY</u>, ANYWAY?

(Inspired by a play called "Who is They?" by Lottie Porch)

Back in the day, they say
Celery will make a lady warm and sweet
Chocolate will make her sassy
But a hat and long gloves will surely make her classy

Or if you have a nightmare
And dream of fish
Somebody's pregnant
Might get their wish (Maybe not!)

Who **is <u>they</u>**, anyway?
Is it people wanting to have their say?
Telling us in a very vivid way
Embellishing the truth each and every day?

They say if you party all night
You'll miss the daylight… Well, they might be right!

They say we got a long row to hoe
'Cause we still trying to do things we can't do no mo'

Well, who *is* **<u>they</u>**, anyway?
Is it Mama, Daddy, Granny or Aunt Bea?
Could be a sign from that gossipy old lady, you see
Telling us how to be you and me.

Like they used to say, the blacker the berry, the sweeter the juice
Or coffee will make you black and loose
Till we found that black is beautiful
We ate a lot of berries,
And drank many cupfuls… of coffee

Some of this wisdom, they say, comes from Proverbs
Only telling it like it was something they already heard,

If a fool who don't know he's a fool, it's okay,
If he did, he wouldn't know it anyway
But a fool who knows he's a fool is dangerous.
Some more sound advice about living, so they say.

Well, who is <u>they</u>, anyway?
They could be you. They could be me.
Always trying to tell you something they think they know
Mostly for sho'
 Like the story 'bout Shine who swam the Atlantic from the Titanic
My mama put her hands on her hip and said, "Now, ain't that a
blip!"

So I say… they could be you… they could be me
Just think of something you can spread
Maybe a tale or two that ain't been said

Then you'll be **they**
And people will listen to what you have to say.

THE BESTEST, SPECIALEST CHRISTMAS EVER

The white fireplace was trimmed with fake red brick. The electric log spun out flickering flames. The top folded out to become a bar that held bottles of Johnny Walker Red, bourbon, and glasses. The sides opened to reveal shelves that held all the necessities of a good party, that Christmas Eve of 1948.

Rab and I sat on the old blue couch waiting for bedtime. Mom decorated our tiny apartment with a live Christmas tree, stockings over the fireplace, and wreaths in the windows. Christmas caressed our home with smells of pecan pies, buttermilk pound cakes, ham, and sweet potatoes. Cookies and milk were sitting on the small mahogany table waiting too… for Santa Claus.

Outside, in the Willert Park Courts, God had sent us the most beautiful snow covering the courtyard, and flakes that rimmed our cold windows. It was so cold, though, as we snuggled together reluctantly, under the homemade quilt. My brother and I were not so friendly and loving at our age. He was five and I was six. But it was necessary.

The next morning, just as the sun shone through shaded windows, we opened our eyes, jumped out of bed… the same bed, stopped in the hallway, peeked at the living room – and exploded with loud piercing screams. Mom was already in the kitchen preparing us grits, livers, gizzards, and biscuits for breakfast – a Christmas special.

Rab saw the train circling all the toys. He clapped and fell down to the floor, looking at his guns and holster and cowboy hat; and a toy soldier because he always wanted to be a cowboy soldier.

I just stood there. Everything was so beautifully spread out in our small space. The cookies were gone. So was the milk. He had certainly been here at our house. I cried "Mama, mama! Santa Claus came last night!" I hugged her, smelling the sweet cinnamon and pecans on her breast.

"Cilla, you were a good girl, and your brother was good, too. Now go on; see what you got. "

"Mama we saw him last night, walking past our bedroom. He had a red suit on."

Mama smiled softly.

Later that morning, after breakfast, our friends started coming over to see what we got for Christmas. We always had the most toys of all the kids. I showed Onell my twin dolls that drank from a bottle and peed! Everyone loved my dollhouse with the tiny people and furniture inside. My friends, Carolyn, Aviva, Faye, Onell, Pat, and Jean brought their dolls with them. All had bright white skin with rosy cheeks and blond hair. Oh, did we love those dolls! Mom gave us cookies and milk as we squealed and laughed and talked about other girls.

Mom played Christmas songs like *"Chestnuts roasting on an open fire..."*

As the excitement of Christmas died down, we became quiet and just sat there hugging our pretty dolls.

Aviva, who was the oldest and smartest of us, said, "Cilla, girl, why you looking so sad? It's Christmas, Jesus' birthday, and look what you got!"

"Viva, I know I should be happy, but I feel a little hurting right here," pointing to my stomach.

"Why? What's the matter? Want me to call your mother?"

All the girls looked at me with puzzled expressions.

"Why did I get so much from Santa Claus? Was I that good? What about Maxie and her sisters and brothers? Did they get something for Jesus' birthday? Last year they got nothing!"

Jean's eyes opened wide, like she was surprised. "W-w-what?" she said, as a tear welled up in her eye.

"'Specially on Christmas, Maxie won't even let us in the door," said Faye.

Just then Viva stood up tall, put her hands on her hips, and as her sister Faye looked on-with her mouth open, said in that deep voice of hers, "Y'all know there ain't no Santa Claus! Were you as good as Maxie this year?"

Silence… *" Tiny tots with their eyes all aglow…"* was all we heard now.

"Is too!" said Pat.

"Is not!" answered Aviva

Mom picked up the record-player needle. My brother, who was in the bedroom with Johnny, came creeping out. They both looked at Aviva, and then my Mom and all of us stared at each other for what seemed like an eternity.

Aviva continued, "Maxie and her brothers and sisters don't get stuff 'cause they family is so poor. Her daddy is always sick from something and her mama can't work 'cause she keeps having them babies."

"Okay, y'all, time to go out and play. Come back tomorrow," Mama said.

Aviva, Faye, Johnny and Bobby braved the blowing snow as they walked to the building next door. The others went upstairs to put their snow gear on and tell their Mamas the new news about Santa Claus.

"Come on. Let's build a snowman," called Johnny.

"Yeah, and bring your sleds, too," answered Bobby.

Rab was always ready to play in the snow. Mama said, "Hey, boy. Put that scarf 'round your neck, before you catch something".

"Mother." She knew something was wrong when I called her that. "Is there really a Santa Claus?"

Rab rolled his big eyes as he slammed the door.

She gave me the best hug; kissed my forehead, and told me almost in a whisper, "I'm your Santa Claus, baby. So is your daddy, your Uncle Burton, his new wife, Merdes, your Aunt Flossie and Miss Kitty. They all your Santa Claus. You got lots of people that love you, and you are a good girl, Cilla."

"But Mama, the cookies and milk? What about the red suit?"

"Me and Miss Kitty ate the cookies and saved the milk. What color is my new coat?"

"Red," I said, still stunned by this surprising news.

"Okay, now: choose something special, something you love – and give it to Maxie."

I looked around. "Except the pee dolls and the doll house," Mama said, with a smile that showed the gap in her teeth.

For Maxie, I chose another doll that I really liked best, some gloves with a scarf and hat, and some Christmas cookies. Mama put one of her pecan pies in the bag and added an envelope with it.

The snow had eased and the sun came out, making the snow sparkle like tiny diamonds.

"Maxie, Maxie, Santa Claus is here," I called. "Open the door!"

As she slowly opened the door, I saw the biggest grin ever, showing those two teeth she lost last week.

Then I heard familiar voices. I saw my friends sitting on the bare floor, eating Christmas cookies, singing, *"All I want for Christmas is my two front teeth."* Christmas presents were spread all over the floor. Later, we were all singing, *"Have yourself a merry little Christmas..."* as we walked home in the sparkling snow.

After dinner that night, we sat around the fireplace and Mom told us about the true story of Santa Claus. She told us how she had house parties several weekends before the holidays. Daddy sent her money, too; so did her friends and family.

"Remember when you stayed the weekend with the Jacksons? Remember when we would call Daddy on the phone to tell him what you and Rab wanted for Christmas?"

Later that night, Mama tucked us in bed.

"Mama," we both said, "this is the bestest, specialest Christmas we ever had."

She smiled, eyes misty as she closed the door. "Go to sleep, if you can. Mama loves you. Next year, I'll tell you 'bout those pretty dolls."

We peeked through the bedroom door and saw most of our friends' mothers, some fathers, and other people. In the background, over the din of their happy voices, we could hear Charles Brown singing, "*St. Nick came down the chimney 'bout half past three, bringing all these pretty presents that you see before me. Merry Christmas, baby. You sho' do treat me niiice.*"

Merry Christmas!

Priscilla Y. Hill (Wiley)
December 17, 2007

OUR WORLD... ONE WORLD

Welcome to our world of the
Grover Cleveland International High School
Our world of many cultures, many religions
And many colors

We are like flowers in an open field
Though some planted in well-shaped gardens
Or prepared and hybridised
Brought here as specially-packaged buds
While others spread freely by the wind

We have assimilated in our own way
Adding our special flavors to the land,
That makes us so unique
As our classrooms celebrate the differences
And help us become aware of the similarities
Of our basic desires to achieve
And live the American dream

Our world is sometimes ostracized, criticized,
Compromised, internalized, politicized, colorized
Publicized, jeopardized and televised on color TV
Or DVD or in the black and white news

We are special because we are educated
In the lessons of the world and
We make knots in the rope that helps
Us to climb higher

We have become doctors, entrepreneurs, labourers,
Law enforcers, politicians, teachers and much more
You can see us in your banks, stores, and schools
Courts, hospitals and in our own businesses

We bring to you a richness of cultures
Spiced with our sunshine, sprinkled with

Our raindrops...
Creating rainbows forever of our
Multinational family.

Cleveland International High School, for those memorable twenty-three years of my life. You helped me grow as a mother, a teacher, an author, and a friend.

     Peace and Love,
     Priscilla Wood Parker
     June, 2003

ODE TO A PEN

I remember the first time I met you. "Please sign in and have a seat until you are called, Miss." I picked you among the many rainbow-colored ones. You were a weird purple with a yellowish-green, curved stripe. When I put you in my hand, you were kind of soft, and I liked you right away.

"Wow, what a beautiful pen," I told the Doctor's secretary. She looked up with a puzzled squint on her face. "May I have it?" I asked her.

"Of course," she said immediately. "We have plenty of them. Take it."

My odyssey begins:

October 26, 2008

Since I've been paying more attention to you, I see more clearly now, and in brilliant colors. You know – I see what I think. WOW! How profound!

October 27, 2008

I am teaching at East High School until January 17. I enlightened two students about my pen in my second-period class. They said you were green. I said yellow, but we agreed you were a mixture of both.

You have created plans for Global Studies, explaining how magnificent the Pyramids are on the Nile River. You have written letters to old friends. You have signed checks to my church and paid a few bills. You have written poetry and helped me finish a short story. Oh, the students thought this was so weird; but it led to a discussion on poetry. We decided to bring our poems and a book to read tomorrow. Do you see how an insignificant thing like a pen can lead to something extraordinary?

October 28, 2008

Well, you are gone now, in an instant! I loaned you to a student who didn't have a pen to see his thoughts. I found another pen from the Holiday Inn; but it was so common, and wouldn't go anywhere I wanted it to go.

I was so happy when the boy gave you back to me. I began to think, "Maybe I'm going a little too far with this project," when I left you in my purse and tried to use a pencil instead. It was worn, unstable and gave off a bland appearance on the paper.

You've got personality and character, but I know one day you will run out and I will have to find another. Then, I will miss you.

October 29, 2008

Where are you? I can't find you anywhere! Did someone take you because they felt they needed you too? Now I will have to use those blue, common, dollar-store pens that are all alike – or try to find a pen as exciting as you have been.

Priscilla Y. Hill
East High School Writing Group

AM I SWEET OR WHAT?

Damn, I got SUGAR!
I've had it a loooong, long time.
Don't even know where it came from.

Did I eat too much sweet stuff growing up?
Did I lick too many cake-batter spoons?
Was it 'cause I sopped up Mom's biscuits
With all that Alaga syrup?

I knew I shoulda backed off
That Peach Cobbler pie,
Especially with the homemade
Ice cream.

Damn, I got SUGAR!

But does it make my body sweet?
Do my kisses taste like creamsicles?
Do I smell like lemon pound cake?
Do my arms wrap around you
Like Lady Fingers?

Damn, I got SUGAR!
But am I sweet or what?

I wrote this poem when my doctor informed me I was a diabetic. At first I was
depressed; then I decided that having "sugar" made me sweet!

May 20, 2004
Priscilla Y. Parker

WILEY'S BOYS' NIGHT OUT

Wiley could hardly wait

'Cause he had a Boys' Night Out date.
Prepared much food the day before
Until his boys came through the door
He cooked chitlins and salad and greens galore
So they wouldn't want to eat ever no more

The girls went out dancing
Having fun and prancing
Thinking 'bout the boys once in a while
As their fingers set and held the dial
But all was merry when they made the call
Hearing the music play, having a ball

The spirits were flying
As they ribbed with fierce lying
They boasted and toasted
Laughed loud as they roasted

There was Buck whose vile sense of humor
Gave Wiley a challenge he could do more
Everyone howled as Buck said out loud
Another "Hey, message?" that made him proud

There was Orell, a new best friend
Joining in the festivities that were about to begin
"Hey, finally a Boys' Night Out!"
He said with a slick smile and a glass of stout

Lloyd, the last who came to play
Trick-or-treating was his forte
Bringing his bag with a rubbery surprise
Made them holler as they opened their eyes

When the girls finally returned
Orell's face seemed a little burned

Buck had that great big grin
And Lloyd was still ribbing agin.

Mr. Hill finally ended his night
But he still wanted to party till broad daylight

Halloween, October 2008

THE IDEAL PLACE

Tonight is a tepid, warm August evening. The New York City skyline shimmers with bright twinkling lights on the dim horizon. I gaze upon the invisible ocean. I know it's there… blue, cold, like this new life has become.

"2, 14, 42, 3, 19, 38, 30…..Damn!" I whispered to myself. Then, "DAMN! That's it!" I shrieked.

The burly, mustached doorman welcomed us reluctantly with a cool, stern, "Good evening, Mr. and Mrs. Hill;" he wanted to add, "What the hell you doing here?" If he only knew…

Our new condo was on the twentieth floor, and would give you vertigo if you didn't watch it. It was located in the east corner of an elegant old building that breathed old dollars and new lottery change (like us).

The gold numbers "2370" were on the door of our fantasy world. The windows on both sides of the living area were long and wide, from the ceiling to the floor, giving us a panoramic view of the ocean and the bright lights of lower Manhattan.

Two steps down on brilliant hardwood floors, a full bar and touch-tone stone fireplace mellowed the room. Ethnic art placed pleasantly around the walls included our favorite music-men sculptures. These delightfully graced our Bose music system, permeating every room with the sounds of Miles and Coltrane's cool jazz.

We kept the red couch that brought the glow and comfort we loved. Bookshelves covered one wall, embracing our collection of books. Multi-colored rugs were scattered in appropriate places; tables and my antique lamps were the right touch. It all came together with the green plants and fresh flowers… on weekly order. It was definitely our dream home, our ideal place…

Looking out into the night, I step onto the veranda, waiting for my man to come home... waiting for the dinner he loves to cook. It's Friday, so I know it will be seafood... crab cakes or lake trout from Baltimore.

The reflection of our warm pool beneath the veranda soothes and beckons me. I wait for him there with prepared Mojitos and Molson Ice. I slide into the water, stroking slowly, then floating, mellowing on my back; seeking the North Star from the Big Dipper. The warmth of the water envelops my body, stirring up old memories. Suddenly I am missing our friends and that old house in Buffalo.

I hear the click of his key and his voice calling me softly, solemnly, "Baby... Baby... I want to go home."

AGING IS A GIFT
(A poem revised from an e-mail sent by a friend)

I am now, for the first time in my life,
the person I've always wanted to be.
And I love me.
Oh, not this body, though,
with wrinkles and sagging butt;
these cottage-cheese hips
looking like my mama in that mirror (still a good thing).

I would never trade family, friends,
Church family for less gray hair,
a flatter belly or more memory.
They are amazing, supportive, spiritual,
faithful, loving,
and keep my secrets safe.

As I age, I've become more kind to myself,
becoming my own best friend.
I don't chide myself for that extra cookie,
or for not making my bed or for buying
that silly-looking hat that I didn't need.

What if I choose to stay up until four a.m.?
to read, play on the computer or watch TV with my man...
and sleep till noon?

So what if I walk on the beach in a swimsuit,
stretched across my bulging body,
no matter who is looking or snickering?
They will get old too someday.

I am blessed to have lived long enough
to have my hair turn gray,
youthful laugh lines forever etched into
deep grooves on my face.

I love being older.
It has set me free.
I like the person I've become.
I'm not going to live forever,
but while I'm here, I will not
waste time complaining of what
coulda, woulda, shoulda been, or worrying
about what will be.

And I shall eat dessert every single day
(If I feel like it!)

My candle burns at both ends;
It will not last the night;
But ah, my foes and oh, my friends –
It gives a lovely light.

Edna St. Vincent Millay 1920

STEP VI   GRANDMA'S CORNBREAD: SERVE WARM, WITH LOVE

Now we've blended and baked all the richest ingredients of spices, special flavors, colors, sprinkled throughout with His Grace and Mercy.

Serve warm and tenderly, with plenty of love. Taste the Joy!

Think of Eloise Worthey Green McPherson, aka Poo-Poo, Weesie, Momma and Grandma's love.

Titus 2:11
"For the Grace of God that brings Salvation has appeared to us all"

THE RECIPE

This recipe is for a large pan because it is so good; you will want to share with friends and neighbors.

2 cups Aunt Jemima cornmeal
2 cups Bisquick or any Baking mix.
1 box Jiffy cornbread mix
1 tsp. salt
4 eggs
½ chopped green pepper
4 oz. jar of pimentos, chopped
8 oz. sharp cheddar cheese
1 can cream style corn
1 can whole corn
Buttermilk; almost a quart, until mixture is however you like

Mix all ingredients well.

Put ¼ cup of oil and ¼ stick of butter in pan and warm in oven until butter is melted.

Pour some of the oil/butter into cornbread mixture; stir until blended.
Make sure you have enough oil to cover the bottom of the pan.

Pour mixture into pan and bake in a 350° oven for 1 hour.
Check with toothpick for doneness. You may have to bake another 15 minutes.

Enjoy!-- Priscilla

Mia Kai Simonne Moody is on her way to Ghana, West Africa!

CONTRIBUTORS' ACKNOWLEDGMENTS

New Covenant United Church of Christ, 459 Clinton Street,
Buffalo, NY 14204;
Rev. Will J. Brown, Pastor.

My Prayer-partner, Marilyn Gault, suggested we ask the
congregation if they would like to make a contribution to this book,
with poems or memoirs of special people and events.
Marilyn's poem about the loss of her brother brought him to life
in our hearts. Marilyn is a hard-working member of our church,
the Treasurer, who helps keep our money safe, and the head of the
committee who brings beauty to our church.

Mrs. Jean Jemison sent us a hand-drawn picture and message. She is
a long-time member and a wonderful artist. She is homebound now,
but has supported our church in any way she could.

Helen Lee submitted loving words about her family members
who have passed on. "Each approached life with their feet planted
firmly on the ground, making them so special to us." Helen's son,
son-in-law and two sisters contributed so much to the creation and
sustenance of New Covenant, as well as Helen herself and brother
Charles Shallowhorn.

Maxine Bennett expressed heartfelt comments about her experiences
at New Covenant UCC. She says, "I have come to realize that
whatever my service to this church has been, it was to please and
honor God, not me." Maxine has been member of many boards,
especially Christian Education, where she has a positive influence
with our children.

Patrick Crosby, a young man pursuing a Career in Media and
Communication, submitted several poems and essays. These
awesome pieces are strong and mind-boggling, about life's
challenges and passion. These essays make us wonder how we, as a
village, helped to raise this young man and make us so proud of him.

Another young lady, who now has graduated from college and is pursuing a higher degree, is Mia Kai Simonne Moody. She wrote a letter to the congregation telling us how she experienced the spirits of ancestors at the edge of the Atlantic Ocean, during her visit to Ghana. Mia is another product of the "Village," who always brings us so much joy.

Then comes a poem by my daughter, Charisse McNeal. She calls it, "Before I knew Jesus, I knew Michael Jackson." This poem is read with the music of "ABC," and truly expresses her feelings about the 70s, early 80s, and Jesus. How about that!

Enjoy and be blessed,
Priscilla

Made in the USA
Lexington, KY
13 August 2012